IRRECONCILABLE
DIFFERENCES

Other Books by the Author

Redemption: The Myth of Pet Overpopulation and the No Kill Revolution in America

Praise for Nathan J. Winograd and Redemption

AWARDS
Silver Medal, Independent Book Publishers Association
Best Book, USA Book News
Muse Medallion, Best Book, Cat Writers Association of America
Award of Excellence, Dog Writers Association of America
First Runner Up, Hoffer Award for Excellence

PRAISE FOR THE BOOK
"*Redemption* is a passionate advocacy for ending the killing of homeless dogs andcats in shelters. Telling the story of how the movement of animal sheltering in the United States was born of compassion and lost its way. . . *Redemption* offers hope that America can yet change its ways. Highly recommended." —*Midwest Book Reviews*

"An important work." —*The Bark magazine*

"Within its pages, readers and animal lovers can find the blueprint not so much for our failure to save the animals in our communities, but for our ability to start doing so today." —*San Francisco Chronicle (SFGate.com)*

"I cannot remember any work that has so dramatically altered my point of view on any subject—nor another book that has me so excited to think of what real reform can do to save the lives of shelter pets." —*Petconnection.com*

"For anyone who has ever loved an animal, this book, like no other non-fiction, takes you through the full spectrum of emotions: from sadness to anger, from fear to hope. But redemption? That is ultimately left up to each and every one of us. . ." —*Air America Radio*

"[A] unique and important book." —*Library Journal*

"[T]he most provocative and best-informed overview of animal sheltering ever written." —*Animal People*

IRRECONCILABLE DIFFERENCES

*The Battle for the Heart & Soul of
America's Animal Shelters*

Nathan J. Winograd

First Edition

Cover and Interior Design: Judith Arisman, arismandesign.com
Cover Photograph: Simone van den Berg, junglefrog.com

Printed in the United States of America

To my wife, Jennifer.

Aside from helping create a better world for animals, she is my other—and foremost—passion in life.

A note about the essays in this book:

Because I wanted each essay to stand on its own, there will be some repetition between them for clarity. This is intentional.

Table of Contents

NO KILL MOVEMENT TIMELINE

1866—(New York City) Henry Bergh launches humane movement with the founding of the American Society for the Prevention of Cruelty to Animals (ASPCA).

1872—(Philadelphia) Women's Humane Society veers off course by becoming the first private humane group to take over the pound.

1888—(New York City) Henry Bergh dies. Against his wishes and justifying his fears that the ASPCA will sabotage its mission, the ASPCA takes over the pound and becomes the leading killer of dogs and cats in New York City.

20th century—(United States) Many humane societies and SPCAs take over pound work and do little more than kill animals.

1971—(Los Angeles) Mercy Crusade opens first municipally funded spay/neuter clinics in the United States. Intakes and deaths plummet, showing killing can be prevented through community-based programs.

1974—(Chicago) Humane Society of the United States, American Humane Association, and the ASPCA have first great meeting of the country's "animal welfare leaders" to discuss "surplus dog and cat problem." The conclusion: "Ownerless animals must be destroyed. It is as simple as that."

1976—(Denver) Humane Society of the United States, American Humane Association, and the ASPCA meet again. In deference to veterinarians who erroneously feared a loss of profits, they discuss and subsequently reject the Los Angeles model of publicly funded low-cost spay/neuter programs despite its documented success; reaffirm policy of killing.

1994—(San Francisco) Under the leadership of Richard Avanzino, San Francisco ends the killing of healthy, homeless dogs and cats in the city, launching the No Kill revolution.

(continued)

1994—(United States) Humane Society of the United States and others begin propaganda campaign to downplay the success of San Francisco.

2001/2002—(Ithaca) Tompkins County, New York, becomes first No Kill community in U.S. history.

2007—(United States)) *Redemption: The Myth of Pet Overpopulation & The No Kill Revolution in America* is published, undermining the claim that killing is necessary and changing the debate nationwide. The number of voices calling for an end to the killing multiplies.

2007-present—(United States) No Kill success spreads nationally. Groups like HSUS are forced to soften their anti-No Kill rhetoric and begin to modify policies which favor killing.

No Kill by the Numbers

How many dogs and cats enter U.S. shelters annually? 8 million.

Of those, how many are savable? Over 90 percent—just over 7 million.

How many savable dogs and cats will actually be saved? 4 million.

How many savable dogs and cats will be killed? 3 million.

Of those killed, how many savable dogs and cats need a new home (i.e., adoption)? If shelters are doing their jobs comprehensively, just over 2 million (3 million on the high end). The remainder includes lost strays who should be reclaimed by their families and feral cats who should be neutered and released.

Other than those who will always adopt from a shelter (those saved above), how many people in the United States are considering a new dog or cat next year who would also consider adoption from a shelter? 17 million. Consequently, even if roughly 80 percent get an animal from a source other than a shelter, killing of healthy and treatable animals can be ended.

Are shelters doing all they can to influence those people to adopt from them? No. A potential adopter writes: "I tried to adopt from my local shelter, but they weren't open on the weekend, it was almost impossible to reach them on the telephone and when I did, I was treated rudely. Nonetheless, I raced down there one day after work, and the place was so dirty. It made me cry to look into the faces of all those animals I knew would be killed. But I found this scared, skinny cat hiding in the back of his cage and I filled out an application. I was turned down because I didn't turn in the paperwork on time, which meant a half hour before closing, but I couldn't get there from work in time to do that. I tried to leave work early the next day, but I called and found out they had already killed the poor cat. I will never go back."

Have any communities adopted their way out of killing? Yes, No Kill communities now exist in all parts of the country.

How long did it take them? They did it virtually overnight when new leadership, committed to the No Kill philosophy and passionate about saving lives, replaced bureaucrats mired in killing.

Why don't shelters do better? A failure of leadership among the national animal welfare groups, a crisis of uncaring among shelter managers, unfettered discretion to avoid putting in place the programs and services that save lives, and the false excuse of "pet overpopulation."

To the Reader

My book *Redemption: The Myth of Pet Overpopulation & The No Kill Revolution in America*, documents how the humane movement, founded on the highest ideals of compassion, devolved into a system of humane societies and other shelters that is the leading killer of dogs and cats in the United States. *Redemption* also shows how in 1994, despite massive opposition from organizations all over the country, the San Francisco Society for the Prevention of Cruelty to Animals (SPCA) spearheaded an effort that achieved the "impossible": saving every healthy homeless dog and cat in the city. In doing so, it fought an entrenched leadership at the San Francisco animal control shelter intent on defending the indefensible status quo, opposition from virtually every shelter director in the contiguous counties, and a propaganda campaign by national animal protection groups threatened by the city's emerging success. But these voices which championed the tradition of killing discounted the very power that assured their defeat: the great love of dogs and cats by San Franciscans and the larger American public.

It has been over a decade since San Francisco's seminal achievement, which launched the No Kill revolution in America. And because
of San Francisco's bold first step, millions of animals across the country
have been saved. Since that time, most of the programs first pioneered
in San Francisco—and ridiculed by the sheltering establishment—have
become more widespread. And, more importantly, other communities
have surpassed even San Francisco's achievement of saving all healthy
dogs and cats by ending the killing of all except hopelessly ill or injured
animals, and vicious dogs with a poor prognosis for rehabilitation.

These communities are saving upwards of 95 percent of all the animals, working to bring "euthanasia" back to its dictionary definition:
"the act or practice of killing or permitting the death of hopelessly sick or
injured individuals in a relatively painless way for reasons of mercy."

As a movement and as a nation, we are increasingly rejecting the consensus of killing and ushering in a new age of compassion and lifesaving
results. And while our work is far from over, and although far too many
animals are still killed in shelters nationwide, we have a genuine solution
to bring that killing to an end. Our focus has now shifted to replacing the
age-old kill-oriented paradigm with one that embraces lifesaving.

But not everyone is celebrating. The status quo always has its champions. The main argument of those who took issue with *Redemption* is my
contention that pet overpopulation is a myth. To discredit the claim, they
have tried to discredit me by arguing that I have some nefarious purpose.
But I did not wake up one day and say, "Pet overpopulation is a myth."
Nor did I think that someday I would champion the notion that it was. I
did not even set out to prove it. It unfolded as part of my work in the humane movement and the facts began to compel further analysis. In fact,
many years ago, I too believed the opposite. I once argued with my wife that
"There were too many animals and not enough homes." I am ashamed of
having done so, but I did. She correctly argued that even if it were true,
killing remained unethical. She also correctly argued that if we took killing
off the table, human ingenuity and human compassion would find a way to
make it work. But, more importantly, she asked me how I knew it was true.

How did I know? *Because I've heard it repeated a thousand times.*
Because I took the fact of killing in shelters and then rationalized the reason

backward. I was too embarrassed to admit so. But therein began a jour-
ney that started in San Francisco, then Tompkins County, New York, then
Charlottesville, Virginia, followed by dozens of shelters in communities
across the country. I reviewed data from over 1,000 shelters nationwide, and reviewed several national studies. And the conclusion became
not just inescapable, but unassailable. Rather than bury it, ignore it or
downplay it, I did what anyone who truly loves animals would have done.
I celebrated it. Why? Because it meant that we had the power to end the
killing, today.

And since that time, other studies have proven I was right; indeed,
they show I was being conservative. Contrary to what many shelters
falsely claim are the primary hurdles to lifesaving (e.g., public irresponsibility or lack of homes), the biggest impediments are actually in shelter
management's hands. Effectiveness in shelter goals and operations begins with caring and competent leadership, staff accountability, effective
programs, and good relations with the community—*which do not currently
exist in most shelters.* It means putting actions behind the words of every
shelter's mission statement that "All life is precious." And it is abun-
dantly clear that the practices of most shelters violate this principle.

Shelter killing is not the result of pet overpopulation; it is the result
of shelter managers who find it easier to kill animals than save them. And
not only do they kill animals they should be saving, too many of them
neglect and abuse them in the process. The bottom line is that shelter
killing is unnecessary and unethical. And pet overpopulation is merely
an excuse for poorly performing shelter managers who want to blame
others for their own failures. Instead of challenging the data, however,
they attack me. But I could go away tomorrow and that wouldn't change
the facts, or the inescapable conclusion. The cat is out of the bag, and is
never going back in.

The No Kill message I advocate is powerful because *it is the truth*
and because it resonates so strongly with the experiences that animal
lovers have with their own brutal and regressive shelters. The combination of substantive data, successful shelters who have embraced No
Kill, and the personal experiences of animal lovers all across the country threaten the champions of the status quo because it does not fit with

their predetermined agenda in support of killing shelters, or in the case of those who actually run shelters, their own killing. Since they cannot attack the message, they are left with attacking the messenger.

They ask the thoroughly unethical question: *How do we stop the movement for a No Kill nation?* When they should be asking: *How can we work to achieve it?* For we have the power to build a new consensus, which rejects killing as a method for achieving results. And we can look forward to a time when the wholesale slaughter of animals in shelters is a cruel aberration of the past. To get to that point, we must learn from history and reject our failures.

In other words, we have to ask—and answer—the question: *What went wrong?* We must first understand how a movement founded on compassion became a network of shelters that do little more than kill animals. Because once we ask that question, we can ask and answer the follow-up: *How do we make it right?*

WHAT WENT WRONG?

An understanding of the No Kill movement and the historical animosity to it by the large, national animal welfare organizations is simply not possible without an understanding of its history. That history reveals that opposition to No Kill by local shelters and national groups like the Humane Society of the United States is not based on any rational philosophy or thoughtful analysis. It is nothing more than an attempt to defray criticism of their own untoward actions over the years; of their unnecessary killing and support of that killing. Consequently, to answer the first question—what went wrong?—we have to look at history for the answer.* We have to go back to the beginning, back to our movement's roots: the founding and incorporation of the nation's first SPCA. We must return to the 19th century, where every summer, the New York City dog pound opened its doors to rid the streets of stray dogs. According to city aldermen, the pound was opened to reduce perceived threats of "nuisance" behavior, rabies, and bite risk. Every day, unclaimed dogs were drowned in a water-tight cistern furnished with a

---

* The following section is an abridged version of my book, *Redemption: The Myth of Pet Overpopulation & The No Kill Revolution in America.*

slatted cover. As many as 80 dogs at a time were drowned, with the largest beaten over the head with a club until they stayed underwater. This was often done in front of a crowd, including neighborhood children.

In 1866, Henry Bergh, a wealthy member of New York City's social aristocracy, incorporated the first SPCA, effectively launching the animal protection movement in the United States. Using the ASPCA as a tool to save animals, Bergh argued that stray dogs posed very little threat to the public health and welfare. His precinct by precinct search found that there were no documented cases in New York City of people contracting rabies from stray dogs. In fighting the city's round up and kill campaign, Bergh succeeded in legislating a series of reforms including: requiring the poundmaster to give dogs fresh food and water, requiring the city to build a new, more modern facility, and passing a law that no one under 18-years-old could turn in dogs to the pound, thereby eliminating what Bergh called the "thieving gangs of young dogcatchers" who were previously paid fifty cents for every dog they brought to the pound, no questions asked. Instead, he advocated that the dogs be left alone as they did not threaten anyone. The reforms succeeded. In just one year, he reduced the number of dogs killed by 84 percent.

LOSING OUR WAY

Tired of fighting Bergh, New York City leaders offered the ASPCA money to run the dog pound. They offered to pay the ASPCA all of its costs for doing so. And they offered to allow the ASPCA to keep any fines it should levy as poundmaster for whatever purpose Bergh saw fit. But Bergh was unmoved. "This Society,"* he said, "could not stultify its principles so far as to encourage the tortures which the proposed give rise to." Henry Bergh was emphatic. His organization was committed to save animals, not to kill them. He would not allow his ASPCA to do the city's bidding and kill dogs they deemed "unwanted."

Toward the end of his life, Henry Bergh often lamented that he hated "to think what will become of the Society when I am gone." Tragically, it

* SPCA is an acronym for "Society for the Prevention of Cruelty to Animals." It is often called either "SPCA" or "Society" for short.

did not take long for his fears to come to pass. Shortly after his death, and against his wishes, the ASPCA capitulated and accepted the pound contract, becoming the city's leading killer of dogs (and later, cats). Within a short period of time, many SPCAs nationwide, modeled after the ASPCA, though independent and distinct, followed suit. The guaranteed income provided by contracts helped sway many of them to abandon their traditional platforms of advocacy and cruelty prosecutions in favor of administering dog control for cities and counties. In many American cities, the pound work was placed in the hands of the local humane society. In doing so, they came up with a three-point plan for animal control:

1. Humane Education: Promoting lifetime commitments and the importance of keeping pets in the house.
2. Adoption: For the first time, some unclaimed animals were offered for adoption.
3. "Humane Death": They introduced the gas chamber to replace slower and more painful ways of killing. (It should be noted that by current standards, there is no real debate about the gas chamber being inhumane. But in the 19th century, activists viewed this as a better alternative than drowning, shooting, and at least in Philadelphia, beating the dogs to death in the public squares.)

With the 1879 founding of the nation's first truly national humane organization, the American Humane Association (AHA), the three-point plan for animal control was embraced and promoted as a national model: *education, adopt some, and kill the rest.* And this platform can be summarized by the 19th century policy of the Animal Rescue League of Boston:

> We keep all dogs we receive, unless very sick or vicious, five days; then those unclaimed are humanely put to death except a limited number of desirable ones for which we can find good homes. We keep from twenty to thirty of the best of the cats and kittens to place in homes and the rest are put to death... We do not keep a large number of animals alive.

By the end of the 19th century, most mainstream humane societies and SPCAs did little more than kill dogs and cats. For the last 100 years, the humane movement's guiding principles mirrored this very mindset, resulting in the deaths of millions of animals every year. Nonetheless, too many communities in the United States are today—in the 21st century—tragically still living under a 19th century model of animal control.

Indeed, until fairly recently, the question of "How can we end the killing?" was not even asked. Instead, what was asked was, "How can we help staff cope with the stress of killing?" "How can we make killing more efficient?" and to their credit, "How can we make it more humane?" But there was little talk of saving lives, little talk of rehabilitating animals, of building foster care networks, of working with rescue groups, of making spay/neuter affordable, of creating a No Kill community even when they had an opportunity to do so.

The first opportunity occurred in Chicago, where in 1974, the Humane Society of the United States, AHA, the ASPCA, the American Veterinary Medical Association, and other self-proclaimed "leaders" met to uncover the "causes" and "solutions" to the "surplus dog and cat problem." But instead of focusing on how the organizations involved could end the killing, the focus became finding someone *else* to blame. And their unanimous conclusion was two-fold.

First, they blamed the animals themselves: their own lack of adoptability required their killing. If they weren't young enough, disliked confinement, or were already bonded to other people (i.e., the family which relinquished them to the shelter), they determined that the animals "must be put down." Accordingly, they concluded that only about 40 percent of shelter animals were "adoptable." That even under ideal circumstances, shelters essentially had an obligation to kill the majority of the animals, including all animals under the age of six weeks as a matter of policy.

Second, they blamed the public. They blasted "pet owners" for inadequately confining their animals. And they pledged to "try to educate the public to the fact that irresponsible companion animal owners are at fault rather than the agencies" actually doing the killing. Accordingly, the solution they embraced had nothing to do with changing their own untoward policies. Instead, they determined that "The only answer will be for the public to become responsible pet animal owners. We must have adequate animal control laws and they must be enforced."

In response, laws were passed across the United States that confined dogs and cats to their homes, required dogs and to a lesser extent cats to be licensed with local authorities, limited the number of animals a family could care for, prohibited feeding stray animals, and provided authority for animal control officers to seize and destroy animals they themselves deemed a "nuisance."

The laws did little to curtail the killing. In fact, they exacerbated it. Not only did shelters set themselves up as adversaries with the public, but at a time when animal shelters were killing most animals, they sought laws to empower themselves to impound, and kill, even more. In addition, shelters began diverting scarce funding—which should have been spent on truly lifesaving programs—to enforcement of laws. Where these laws were passed, kill rates tended to increase as a result.

The historical legacy of taking over the pound work for municipalities, and blaming and punishing the public while killing the animals, has been a shift in our nation's SPCAs and humane societies from Henry Bergh's *animal welfare* to an *animal control* orientation, favored by the abusive city dog catchers he fought. Ed Duvin, an early critic of this shift, described it succinctly:

> Historically, SPCAs made the tragic mistake of moving from compassionate oversight of animal control agencies to operating the majority of kill shelters. The consequences in terms of resource allocation and sacrificing a coherent moral foundation have been devastating.

Put more bluntly, when the ASPCA took over the pound contract in New York City following Henry Bergh's death, it began a century of squandering not only his life work, but more significantly the ASPCA's vast potential. Bergh's ideal of a humane agency founded to save animals was replaced with shelters across the country whose primary purpose was—and remains—killing animals, whether or not they are suffering. And for most of the animals "rescued" by these agencies, death remains a totally unnecessary, but virtual certainty. As a result, compassion became control. And shelter animals are needlessly killed by the millions. The approach did not work then. It does not work now. A new approach is needed.

A NEW AGE DAWNS

At the time of the 1974 Chicago conference when HSUS, the ASPCA, and others forged a punitive, ineffective agenda of killing, a more effective and humane approach was already in existence. In 1971, Mercy Crusade of Los Angeles, a local humane group, opened the first municipally funded spay/neuter clinic in the United States for the companion animals in low income households. The public's participation was so overwhelming that in 1973, two additional clinics opened and by 1979, a fourth was created. At a time when many cities were growing and seeing increases in the number of animals impounded, Los Angeles City shelters were taking in roughly half the number of animals than before the clinics opened, while killing per capita was reduced to the lowest third of U.S. cities.

Unfortunately, in a round of budget cuts, the clinics were closed and Los Angeles began to follow the "Chicago model" of sheltering. In the year 2000, the General Manager of Los Angeles Animal Services proposed the nation's toughest animal ordinance to punish perceived "irresponsible pet owners"; in 2008, they passed an even tougher one which increased killing by roughly 30 percent. No effort was made to reopen the spay/neuter clinics that brought impounds and deaths to all-time lows. And not surprisingly, Los Angeles remains a battleground between No Kill advocates and the pound, with tens of thousands of animals needlessly losing their lives every year.

But the lesson ignored by subsequent leaders in Los Angeles—never mind the laws, the answer lies in high-volume, low-cost spay/neuter and other community based services—was learned by someone else. It is a model embraced and vastly expanded by Richard Avanzino, then President of the SPCA in San Francisco. When Avanzino took over the San Francisco SPCA, it was the acting poundmaster for the City and County of San Francisco, a role it held for nearly a century. Not surprisingly, like its counterpart in New York City and hundreds of other American cities, it was the leading killer of animals in its community. Indeed, over 20,000 animals were being impounded annually, with the vast majority put to death.

In 1989, Avanzino gave up the animal control contract, returning it to the city, which built and ran its own shelter. Instead of killing, the San Francisco SPCA went back to its roots, focusing on programs that save the

lives of animals. In the process, Avanzino pioneered a bold series of programs and services to end the killing of savable dogs and cats, including
the nation's first offsite adoption venues, foster care, behavior and training
for shelter animals, non-lethal alternatives for feral cats, and more. Like
Los Angeles of the 1970s, intakes were cut in half to about 13,000 per year.
Along with the feral cat program, comprehensive adoption efforts, and the
medical and behavior initiatives, the deaths of healthy dogs and cats in any
San Francisco shelter (including the city pound) fell to a trickle.

Emboldened, Avanzino was ready to take the city (even with animal control "kicking and screaming" in opposition) to the next bold
step: a lifesaving guarantee for each and every healthy dog and cat in San
Francisco, no matter which shelter they entered, no matter how many
there were, and no matter how long it took to find them a home. During
the next decade, deaths of dogs and cats overall (healthy, treatable, and
feral) plummeted—an achievement unparalleled anywhere in the country—with the number of healthy dogs and cats killed falling to zero. It was
a monumental, unprecedented achievement and should have inspired
nationwide celebration by shelter directors and their large, national allies like HSUS. That is what one would expect from organizations and
their leaders who claim to be dedicated to saving animals. But they did
not celebrate. Concerned that San Francisco's meteoric success would
expose their own failures, they attacked.

As part of their misinformation campaign to downplay San Francisco's achievement, shelter managers and national leaders made numerous untrue claims: they claimed San Francisco's success was merely "smoke
and mirrors," they claimed the animals were surreptitiously killed and not
counted in statistics, they claimed that No Kill actually led to more killing. When animal lovers in other communities ignored those arguments
and demanded similar success, the architects of the status quo—the heads
of the ASPCA, HSUS, and regressive shelters nationwide—shifted tactics.
Rather than claiming that San Francisco's success was a fabrication, they
tried to isolate it by arguing that San Francisco was so unique, its success
required a very specific set of circumstances that did not exist elsewhere.

Roger Caras, the President of the ASPCA, argued that success in San
Francisco was due to a large gay population: "Running on and on about

no-kill as the answer is maybe okay in San Francisco, with a population of 70,000, one third who are gay (the gay community is traditionally the most animal friendly)." Not only is the claim specious, but Caras downplayed the population of San Francisco over ten-fold. At the time, it was roughly 750,000 people. Moreover, he conveniently ignored New York City's own thriving gay community. Indeed, the birthplace of the modern gay rights movement in the United States was not San Francisco, but New York City.

Not to be outdone, leadership at Los Angeles County's Department of Animal Care and Control argued that the only reason why San Francisco succeeded was because animals could not enter the city from other parts of the state because it was "surrounded by water." Although certainly inventive, a casual glance at any map will show that the city is not an island, but a part of the continental United States.

But by far, the most common argument against taking San Francisco's success as a replicable model was that San Francisco was an "educated" and "urban" community, and that similar success in rural American would be impossible with a "less educated" and "less progressive" populace. Ironically, it was the leadership of rural shelters making these claims.

THE REVOLUTION SPREADS

At the time, San Francisco was not only saving healthy dogs and cats, it was a whisper away from extending the guarantee to sick and injured but treatable animals as well. Unfortunately, Avanzino moved on to other pursuits and subsequent leadership at the San Francisco SPCA, who came from traditional shelters and was schooled in the old-maxims, had different priorities. The new President and his hand-picked acolytes and successors curtailed or dismantled the nuts and bolts programs that brought San Francisco death rates to national all-time lows.

At the time, I was the Director of Operations for the San Francisco SPCA. And as to the question of whether or not No Kill could be accomplished in a rural community, I believed it was time to find out. After waging a losing battle against my boss and the Board of Directors to keep the SPCA focused on its No Kill mandate, I left the organization to run the open-admission Tompkins County SPCA in upstate New York, taking the No Kill philosophy to a largely rural community—and, more importantly, taking the model to an animal control shelter, with programs and services pioneered by San Francisco which I've come to call the No Kill Equation. These programs include:

- Comprehensive adoption opportunities including incentives, weekend and evening hours, and offsite adoption venues;
- Foster care for underaged animals, those not ready for adoption, those who may need more focused care, and when space at the shelter is at a premium;
- Socialization and behavior care and rehabilitation efforts to keep or to get dogs and cats happy and healthy;
- Thorough cleaning and care standards so animals do not get sick;
- Medical care and rehabilitation as prevention and for care of already ill/injured animals;
- Working with rescue groups;
- Trap-Neuter-Release (TNR) programs for feral and other free-roaming outdoor cats;
- Helping people overcome behavior, medical or environmental conditions that cause them to relinquish animals;
- Proactive efforts to help reunite lost pets with their families; and,
- An effective public relations strategy so that shelters effectively compete with commercial sources of animals.

The results were dramatic. Although the shelter impounded animals for all ten towns and municipalities of Tompkins County, impounded rabies-suspect animals for the Tompkins County Health Department, enforced state animal cruelty laws and local ordinances, and enforced dangerous dog laws, in 2001-2, Tompkins County went from a community that

- Was killing healthy dogs and cats to killing none;
- Was killing treatable sick and injured dogs and cats to killing none;

- Was killing feral cats to killing none;
- Reduced the death rate by 75 percent; and,
- Increased the total save rate to 93 percent, well beyond San Francisco (in fact, Tompkins County has saved at least 92 percent of the animals every year for the last seven years).

Not only did the Tompkins County SPCA find homes for all the "cute and cuddly" kittens and puppies in the shelter; it also found homes for all the savable animals who were old, deaf, blind, missing limbs, unweaned, and traumatized. In the process, Tompkins County became the safest community for homeless animals in the United States and the nation's first—and at the time, only—No Kill community, saving all healthy animals (including other animals such as rabbits, hamsters, gerbils, mice, ferrets, birds, "farm" animals, and reptiles), treatable animals, and feral cats. Once again, a nationwide celebration should have followed.

And once again, sadly, it did not. In fact, entrenched shelter directors across the country were overcome by collective amnesia. When San Francisco became the first city in the country saving all healthy dogs and cats, they said: "You can do it in an urban community, but you can't in a rural one." When Tompkins County achieved No Kill success in rural America, they argued the opposite: "You can do it in a rural community, but not in an urban one." At the same time, the large, national organizations simply ignored it. To this day, neither HSUS nor the ASPCA has ever published a single article saying No Kill has been achieved.

It is like No Kill had not been achieved. It was treated as if the key to ending the killing remained undiscovered. The nation's most influential animal welfare organizations ignored the only effective model at ending the killing of savable animals in shelters. But when ignoring it failed, when downplaying it failed, shelter managers recycled the fiction they used about San Francisco: any success in Tompkins County was unique to a very specific set of largely geographical circumstances. In other words, "You might be able to do that in New York and California," they cried, "but you could not achieve it anywhere else," most of all—they said—in the "backward" South.

But one Southerner noted what was happening in Tompkins County, and after visiting the shelter, she decided she was going to find a job running a shelter and ultimately did. Despite, or perhaps because she had no prior shelter experience, she implemented the model at the animal control facility in Charlottesville, Virginia she was now in charge of. A newcomer to animal control, she took over a shelter widely criticized by the rescue community for overkill and poor care of the animals. A shelter, like the others, that relied on the fiction of too many animals and not enough homes, and that it had no choice but to adopt a few, and kill the remainder. Like Avanzino, and like myself, Susanne Kogut was not schooled in the paradigm of killing, and she was deeply committed to the No Kill philosophy. Not surprisingly, she reduced deaths by half in her first year, saving roughly 87 percent of the animals. The following year, she saved 92 percent. Her agency has now been No Kill for three years.

Predictably, the "catch and kill" sheltering establishment did not celebrate the success. And they came up with yet another reason why it was not replicable, arguing that No Kill was not possible in communities shifting from a rural to an urban economy, with rapidly expanding populations because the influx of new people would bring more animals, and that, in turn, would quickly overwhelm the infrastructure of animal control, forcing them to kill.

But when the model succeeded virtually overnight in Washoe County, Nevada—one of the fastest growing communities (Reno) in one of the country's fastest growing states—that argument was quickly proven false. A new director, following the No Kill Equation model of sheltering doubled adoptions, cut kill rates in half and achieved a roughly 90 percent rate of lifesaving for both dogs and cats, despite a per capita intake rate twice the national average, over three times higher than the City of Los Angeles, and five times the rate of San Francisco's.

And today, there are many other No Kill communities: in Kentucky, in Indiana, in Colorado, in California, in Utah, and elsewhere and the rate of success is increasing exponentially. While these communities are economically, geographically, and demographically diverse, each of them shares the most important ingredient for success: a hard-working,

compassionate animal shelter director not content to kill, while passing the blame to others. San Francisco would still be killing at an astonishing rate if not for Richard Avanzino. As would Tompkins County,
Charlottesville, Reno, and all the other No Kill communities. Individual
leaders make—or break—the lifesaving initiative. With no allegiance to the
status quo, with no faith in conventional wisdom, these directors reject
the defeatist excuses of why it cannot be done in their communities. And
they have succeeded in the most important job a shelter has: saving lives.

THE MYTH OF PET OVERPOPULATION

So why is killing still happening in other communities? Is it because
there are too many animals? Not enough homes? Irresponsible people?
Is it because we don't have enough mandatory laws? Is it because the animals aren't "adoptable"?

We have been conditioned to believe those excuses. But plenty of
communities prove otherwise. And so does the data nationally. Every
year, well over 20 million people are looking to bring a new dog or cat
into their home, more than the total number of dogs and cats entering
shelters. Some are already committed to adopting from a shelter. Others
are committed to going elsewhere. But of the total, 17 million have not
decided where they will get their companion animal, and research shows
they can be influenced to adopt from a shelter.

Furthermore, not all animals entering shelters need adoption:
Some are lost strays who will be reclaimed by their family (shelters
which are comprehensive in their lost pet reclaim efforts, for example, have demonstrated that as many as two-thirds of stray dogs can be
reunited with their families). Others are unsocialized feral cats who
should be neutered and released to their habitats. Some will be vicious
dogs or are irremediably suffering and will, unfortunately, be killed at
this time in history. In the end, a shelter needs to find new homes for
roughly half of all incoming animals. If shelters increase their market
share by three percent (replacement homes and expanding homes), we
would be a No Kill nation today. In other words, 17 million people are
potentially vying for the roughly three million available dogs and cats

whose lives are at risk at shelters across this country, but for adoption. Even if roughly eight out of ten got their animal elsewhere, we could still zero out the killing.

The problem, therefore, is not too many; the problem is a lack of lifesaving programs for all the categories of animals entering shelters and poor efforts in finding homes for animals who need one. From poor customer service, to a lack of weekend and evening hours, to dirty facilities, to under-performing staff, to a lack of marketing, to a failure to do offsite adoptions, to exorbitant fees, SPCAs and animal control agencies across the country are not run effectively, efficiently, or humanely, and thus are needlessly killing animals.

Instead of a No Kill nation, we have this tragic scenario faced by a potential adopter, an all-too-common example of betrayal in our nation's shelters:

> I tried to adopt from my local shelter, but they weren't open on the weekend, it was almost impossible to reach them on the telephone and when I did, I was treated rudely. Nonetheless, I raced down there one day after work, and the place was so dirty. It made me cry to look into the faces of all those animals I knew would be killed. But I found this scared, skinny cat hiding in the back of his cage and I filled out an application. I was turned down because I didn't turn in the paperwork on time, which meant a half hour before closing, but I couldn't get there from work in time to do that. I tried to leave work early the next day, but I called and found out they had already killed the poor cat. I will never go back.

It is not pet overpopulation that is killing animals when shelter directors willfully refuse to implement lifesaving alternatives to killing; such as when neonatal kittens are killed because the shelter does not have a comprehensive foster care program, as is too often true in shelters across the country. Similarly, it is not pet overpopulation to blame when adoptions are low because the shelter isn't doing offsite adoptions. It is not pet overpopulation when animals are killed because working with rescue groups is downplayed, discouraged, or these groups aren't given access to animals facing death. It is not pet overpopulation to blame when feral cats are killed because a TNR program is not in place. It is not pet overpopulation when people aren't helped to overcome behavior, medical or environmental conditions that cause them to relinquish animals because effective pet retention programs aren't implemented. It is not pet overpopulation to blame when animals are killed because of ineffective and passive efforts to help reunite lost pets with their families. It is not pet overpopulation to blame when shy or scared dogs are killed because a rehabilitation program has not been integrated into the behavior assessment process. It is not pet overpopulation to blame when adoptions aren't steadily increasing because an effective public relations strategy and adoption campaign isn't being coordinated, or the shelter is not effectively competing with commercial sources of animals. It is not pet overpopulation to blame when dogs go "cage crazy" because volunteers aren't welcome or allowed to socialize them, and then "cage crazy" dogs are killed because behavior rehabilitation efforts are not in place. It is not pet overpopulation to blame when cats get sick because shelter staff are not thorough in their cleaning and thoroughly reprimanded for failure to do so. It is not pet overpopulation to blame when these sick cats are killed because the shelter doesn't provide medical care or treatment. And it is especially not pet overpopulation to blame when animals are killed despite empty cages, an all-too-common occurrence in shelters across the country that are killing and claiming to do so because of "lack of space."

In fact, we could be a No Kill nation today. But we aren't. And we aren't for one reason and one reason only—shelter managers find killing easier than doing what is necessary to stop it. Accordingly, we must reject the term "euthanasia" to describe unnecessary shelter killing. We must stop using the term "pet overpopulation" when it does not exist. We must stop portraying the problem as the fault of the public when shelter managers fail to implement the necessary programs. And we need to stop seeking laws that empower animal control to impound and kill more animals.

This is the political cover that allows local governments to underfund their shelters, as well as to appoint and retain people who have no business holding the power of life and death. This is the political cover that gives shelter directors the *carte blanche* they need to kill, and prevents even animal lovers in a community from demanding an immediate end to the bloody mess. Shelters are supposed to be the safety net for animals, just as are other social service agencies, which also deal with human irresponsibility. By contrast, they don't use that as an excuse to negate their own in failing to implement necessary programs to respond effectively and humanely. Imagine if Child Protective Services took in abused, abandoned and unwanted children—then killed them. We should no more tolerate it for animals.

The fact that pet overpopulation is a myth, however, doesn't mean our work is done. It doesn't mean we should not promote spay/neuter. It doesn't mean some people are not irresponsible. But it *does* mean that our efforts to end the killing must be strategic responses to what is *actually* killing animals and not phantoms of our movement's unfounded dogmas. While people surrender animals to shelters, it is the shelter that kills them. And one does not necessarily follow or excuse the other.

There is a great hypocrisy in the humane movement. While shelters decry the public's irresponsibility, shelters reject responsibility for the animals in their care. And while they tell the public not to treat the animals as disposable, they treat animals exactly that way by killing them—and literally disposing of their bodies in landfills. In fact, they will even deny that they are killing. The Humane Society of the United States held a workshop on "euthanasia" at their national sheltering conference in March of 2006. According to the speaker,

> We're not; we're not killing them... in that "kill" is such a negative connotation. It's... we're not *killing* them. We are taking their life, we are ending their life, we are giving them a good death, we're humanely destr—whatever. But we're *not killing*. And that is why I cannot stand the term "No Kill shelters."

Animal shelter professionals from coast-to-coast applauded in agreement, but more disturbing is the nation's "euthanasia" expert professing an Orwellian logic: killing is not killing, killing is kindness. And when you deny all responsibility, the impetus to change your own behavior disappears.

There are communities in the United States that have eliminated population control killing. We want—and the animals deserve—No Kill in every city in the country. But it requires shelter leaders committed to these goals and embarking on a campaign of diligent implementation.

That is where we must focus our efforts at reform. Only the No Kill Equation model has achieved this success. It is a program model which changes the way shelters operate and which gives the animal loving public an integral role in that operation. If a community wants success, this is the way to go: nothing else has succeeded.

Trying to achieve a new end with a failed model doesn't make sense. It is, in fact, the very definition of insanity: of doing the same thing over and over and expecting different results. It would be like having a loved one in a hospital and dying, and the doctor comes in and says:

> We can give a modern treatment that has worked every time it has been given so long as the prescription is followed. Or, we can give a treatment that was developed in the 19th century and has never had success, but is very popular.

This is the choice we face in animal sheltering today.

But when animal lovers challenge the status quo, as they are increasingly across the country, they are labeled "divisive." They are told by entrenched shelter directors, the uncaring bureaucrats who oversee them, and the leaders of the large, national groups who have taken on for themselves the role of defending poorly performing shelters, that No Kill is impossible (though it has already been achieved in numerous communities). And they'll use that as an excuse to whitewash their failures to hold staff accountable or their failure to implement lifesaving programs; to fill body bags, despite empty cages.

As I wrote in *Redemption*,

> The truth is we are not a unified movement, nor are we even the same movement. We were not part of the same movement when Henry Bergh, the founder of the nation's first SPCA, fought the dogcatchers of New York City. We were not part of the same movement when Richard Avanzino fought an entrenched animal control bureaucracy in San Francisco. We were not the same movement when the Humane Society of the United States argued that caring for feral cats was tantamount to animal abandonment in North Carolina. And we are not part of the same movement today. No Kill advocates, on the one hand, and kill-oriented traditionalists, on the other, are on a collision course.

In the two years since *Redemption's* publication, there has been a sea change of public opinion, with tens of thousands of animal lovers rejecting the paradigm of killing in U.S. shelters. And it is that rejection of the status quo, propelled by the American public's great love of companion animals, which is explored in this book's essays.

This is the *ongoing and evolving* story of animal sheltering in the United States, a movement that was born of compassion and then lost its way. It is the story of the No Kill movement, which says we can and must stop the killing. It is about a social movement as noble and just as those that have come before. Above all, it is a story about believing in the community and trusting in the power of compassion.

Why Are the Cages Empty?

It is the height of the summer kitten season in an Oregon shelter where seven out of ten cats are losing their lives. More cats and kittens will enter the shelter during this time of year than any other period. The director says he has no choice but to kill them: there are too many, and he simply does not have "the space." I visit expecting every cage to be full. But only six cages in the adoption room have cats. Forty-six of them, the remainder, are empty. Why?

The Louisiana shelter I visit has one of the highest death rates for cats in the country: 92 percent of all cats who enter the facility are killed. The excuse: "lack of space." Once again, I enter the shelter expecting to see cats and kittens in every available cage. I enter one room: every cage is empty. I enter a second room: every cage is empty. How many cats are available for adoption I ask? The answer: one. Why?

The Philadelphia Department of Public Health proclaims that its animal control shelter is run by a caring and well-trained staff, and the killing they do (roughly 22,000 of the 25,000 animals they receive annually) is inevitable,

due to lack of space. On the day I arrive, animals are being killed. I count the
number of empty cat cages: 70. Every other dog kennel is also empty. Why?

WE ARE A nation of dog and cat lovers. But our nation's shelters are killing roughly four million of them yearly. And for far too long, we have been told that the killing is exclusively the public's fault; that shelters—through no fault of their own—merely perform the public's dirty work, with skill, compassion, and dedication.

Most people believe that animal shelters find homes for as many animals as they can, and gently "euthanize" the rest because there is no other choice. Many people believe that if there were alternatives, shelters would not kill because they are staffed with benevolent animal lovers, laboring against overwhelming odds and offering a humane death only when necessary. Because we could not do it, we assume they do it because they have no choice.

These shelters and their large national allies—the Humane Society of the United States, the ASPCA, and the National Animal Control Association—encourage this belief. Accordingly, they claim that leadership and staff at every one of these agencies "have a passion for and are dedicated to the mutual goal of saving animals' lives."

It is this portrayal that silences criticism of shelters, the vast majority of which have a paltry number of adoptions and staggeringly high rates of killing. The public is told, "We are all on the same side," "We all want the same thing," "We are all animal lovers," and criticism of shelters and staff is unfair and callous because "No one wants to kill." Therefore, a large national organization can boldly publish, without the slightest hint of sarcasm or irony, a picture of a puppy—a young, healthy, perfectly adoptable puppy—put to death with the accompanying caption: "This dog was one of the lucky ones who died in a humane shelter... Here caring shelter workers administer a fatal injection."

These groups tell us repeatedly that our nation's animal shelters are staffed by animal lovers who hate to kill and would do anything in their power to protect animals and save their lives. The facts, however, tragically and frequently tell a very different story.

BUREAUCRATIC INDIFFERENCE

Since many of the agencies contracting to perform animal control come with the label "Humane Society" or "Society for the Prevention of Cruelty to Animals," the assumption is that these shelters are operating humanely and staffed by directors and employees committed to animal protection. In reality, agencies that may have initially been founded by people with enormous dedication to animal welfare lost focus when these organizations took over the "pound contracts" from the cities and towns in which they reside. Consequently, killing became the agencies' central strategy, and working in an animal control shelter was no longer a "mission," but a job. In fact, neither compassion nor passion for saving lives is needed for employment as an animal control director. A shelter director need not prove lifesaving success; only experience running other animal control shelters. The fact that a director oversaw a shelter that killed the vast majority of the animals in its care does not end the director's career. The most important question—"How successful were you at saving lives?"—is rarely asked. Not surprisingly, while many of these organizations have become very large and influential, they have also become bureaucratic, lacking the zeal for reform that characterized the movement's early founders.

In some communities, animal control shelters are placed under the rubric of health departments. These shelters are not focused on saving lives but tend to focus primarily, if not exclusively, on "public health." Too often, they take an expansive definition of "public health" that views animals as little more than disease threats. Other times, these agencies are placed under the umbrella of police departments. These shelters relegate lifesaving to the sidelines as they tend to focus primarily, if not exclusively, on "public safety." A stray dog is less an animal who needs to be rescued and more a potential threat of a bite that must be eradicated. And, tragically, some agencies are supervised by sanitation departments. What does this say about a government's commitment and view of animal sheltering and the priorities of the bureaucrats who oversee and staff these facilities? In fact, it shows that the county considers strays to be akin to "trash" that must be "picked up" and thrown "away."

At the same time, the large national animal protection organizations that do shelter assessments, promote model policies, hold national conferences, and offer supportive advocacy to shelters should ensure that they are operated in the most humane way possible. Tragically, they do not because they are staffed by the people who have risen from the ranks of similar killing shelters and bring the same mindset with them when they go to work for these national organizations. As a result, not a single progressive national voice historically spoke on behalf of saving the animals in shelters. There has been little accountability, little innovation, and almost complete hegemony over the national discourse that argues that killing is kindness—all of which have conspired to cement a crisis of uncaring in our nation's animal shelters.

Across the United States, public and private shelters are not doing enough to save lives. They are not run compassionately, effectively, or in a manner that maximizes lifesaving. Tragically, until very recently, most animal advocates failed to demand the resignation of such directors. And at the core of this failure are long-standing and historic misperceptions about both the reasons why animals are being killed in shelters, and the motivation of the people who carry out the killing. The notion that most shelter directors and their staff share the same goals and values as animal advocates in the community has for too long stifled criticism and, as a result, prevented needed and true reform.

THE BUCK STOPS HERE

Why are some shelters still killing in the face of alternatives, while others save all but hopelessly ill animals? One common excuse is that shelters with higher rates of lifesaving are somehow "unique." But this excuse ignores the fact that each community that has experienced No Kill success was, at one time, as regressive as those that continue killing.

Why do some shelters send thousands of animals every year into foster care, while other shelters do not? Indeed, one such shelter fired volunteers who took motherless newborn kittens home and bottle-fed them until they were old enough to eat on their own and be adopted. Why do some shelters seek out rescue groups, while other shelters kill animals these groups are offering to save? Why do some shelters neuter and release feral cats, while others not only oppose such efforts, but send officers out to write citations to cat lovers who do?

The answer is simple: the most important factor that determines community success in saving lives—or ending them—is the person who runs the animal control or large private shelter in a community, and that person's commitment—or lack thereof—to implementing the needed lifesaving programs. That is why a 2009 national study by the No Kill Advocacy Center found that rates of lifesaving were not determined by rates of funding. One shelter saved 90 percent of the animals despite spending $1.50 per capita on animal control. Another saved only 40 percent while spending $6.00 per capita, four times the rate of the first. One community has seen killing rates increase over 30 percent despite having one of the best funded shelter systems in the nation. Another has reduced death rates by over 50 percent despite cutting costs. Ultimately, the difference between those shelters which are succeeding and those which continue to fail is not the size of the budget, but the commitment of its leadership.

While communities should provide adequate funding, merely throwing money at the problem will do very little without leadership committed both to lifesaving and to accountability. In King County, Washington, the County Council has spent millions of additional dollars since three independent evaluations in 2007 and 2008 revealed high rates of illness, deplorable conditions, and systematic neglect at King County Animal Care & Control (KCACC). In fact, until recently, the King County Council has never denied a funding request for KCACC. Despite the allocation of millions of additional dollars, animals continue to languish, continue to get sick because of poor care, continue to go untreated, continue to suffer, and continue to be killed needlessly. In other words, the difference in lifesaving rates between shelters is determined by the choices made by the people running them. All the money in the world won't save dogs and cats in shelters run by directors who simply refuse to implement alternatives to killing. And when it comes to the shelters whose directors are killing large numbers of animals, those choices and priorities manifest themselves not only in their appalling kill rates, but also in the poor and oftentimes cruel treatment the animals in their facilities must endure.

IN-HUMANE SOCIETIES

In the last several years, I've been hired to evaluate dozens of shelters nationwide. These shelters were expecting my arrival, and their staff should have been operating at their personal and professional best. I should have found clean kennels, attentive staff, and well cared for animals. Instead, I found this:

In a Georgia shelter, a dog with a bloody club foot (missing all toes) was impounded by a field officer who did not report or document the injury, nor did he bring it to the attention of supervisors. Since the shelter relied on prison labor to cut costs and oversight was lax, no one came forward to provide care. As a result, by the time I arrived for an assessment, the dog had been languishing injured—and in pain—for several days, before being killed. Two weeks prior, cats housed in an outdoor "pen" died of hypothermia due to freezing temperatures at night. No one was disciplined. No one was fired.

In a Maryland shelter, a dog with a broken leg languished with no medical care or pain relief for five days, and was killed upon my arrival.

In a Washington shelter, a dog who could not stand and was bleeding profusely failed to receive remedial care or pain relief of any kind; while cats in the infirmary were not given any food or water during a holiday weekend when the shelter was closed to the public.

A Missouri shelter had an overwhelming smell that made it difficult, if not unhealthy, to breathe. Meanwhile, filthy conditions produced epidemics of respiratory infections. The shelter then claimed it had "no choice" but to kill the cats "because they are sick."

In a Texas shelter, kittens in the infirmary were left without food and fresh water for extended periods, while nursing puppies have been flushed down trench drains and drowned.

These are not examples of a bygone era; nor are they aberrations. All occurred in the last several years at shelters that claimed commitment to lifesaving and high quality services. And all mimic complaints about shelters I have received from animal lovers all over the country. One shelter killed approximately 22,000 of the 25,000 dogs and cats it annually took in. It was even killing "for space" on a day it had over seventy empty cages because killing was quicker and easier than cleaning cages and providing care. Despite this, both the ASPCA and the Humane Society of the United States said that this particular shelter's deplorable levels of killing were within the "norms" of U.S. shelters. What progressive animal advocates in that community called a "slaughterhouse," national animal welfare organizations called "norms."

With such low expectations from the large national organizations that people turn to for guidance, is it any wonder that we have accepted that the best we can do for homeless animals is to adopt a few and kill the rest? Is it any wonder that national groups have fooled the public into believing that killing is done at the hands of caring shelter workers who would do everything in their power, leave no stone unturned, implement any program, if it held a promise of something different?

Shelters kill because killing is easier than implementing needed programs. Shelters kill because incompetence, uncaring, and neglect of animals are, unfortunately, endemic and epidemic in our nation's animal shelters.

But until recently, few in the animal protection movement have been willing to recognize this reality, or to state such facts publicly. Critics who do are attacked as "divisive." Indeed, it is a common notion in the animal protection movement that if we could all set our differences aside and "get along," we would better serve the animals. But how can this be so when there are those staffing traditional humane societies and shelters who hold viewpoints and act in ways which are the antithesis of the very goals—saving lives, doing no harm, and advancing the rights of animals— that the animal protection movement exists to promote? Why should we remain silent and complacent about their failures simply because they claim to be part of our movement and to care about animals, even when their actions oppose such values and priorities? Movement unity and cohesion do not—and should not—supersede our duty to animals and the goals we seek on their behalf.

While it is always more difficult and uncomfortable to stand up to one's so-called "friends" than to stand up to one's "enemies," stand up we must. For if we are ever to achieve a No Kill nation—and end the wholly unnecessary killing of millions of animals every year in U.S. shelters—we must respond strategically to the actual problems that cause animal suffering and prevent greater lifesaving. And the biggest impediment to No Kill is that many who currently oversee our nation's animal shelters do not care and therefore eschew their duties to animals.

Nationwide lifesaving success will be achieved only when all shelters and all animal protection groups embrace the No Kill paradigm that says that the killing in our nation's shelters must end—and not when we "respect" opposing views that accept and legitimize that killing. To the extent that shelter bureaucrats and their national allies oppose the No Kill philosophy, animals will continue to needlessly die. To the extent that animals continue to die needlessly, we are morally bound to speak out on their behalf. Now that we know the key to ending the killing, our silence amounts to betrayal. The humane movement must acknowledge that animals in shelters have a right to live. And that will occur only when we speak loudly and clearly in their defense, and reject the viewpoints that have historically blocked No Kill's widespread implementation.

TIME FOR CHANGE

It has been over a decade since communities with compassionate animal directors have achieved success at saving lives. Most of our country's shelter directors have chosen to ignore that proven success, while digging in their heels and disparaging the No Kill philosophy. Others have responded to public pressure by putting forth bold claims and promising success in five years in order to silence critics and delay accountability, yet they are failing to implement the programs to make such promises a reality. Instead, the business of killing in their shelters continues. For over a decade, the energy and resources to achieve No Kill success in their own shelters have been squandered on fighting and denigrating the success of others. The time has come for animal advocates to reclaim these organizations.

Consequently, the crucial first step in achieving a No Kill nation is regime change. It is time to demand the resignation of those shelter directors who reject the No Kill philosophy. Ultimately, these shelter managers act in our name: they are killing with our taxes, with our donations, as agencies representing us, and they are even blaming us (and our neighbors) by claiming the public's irresponsibility leaves them with no other choice. And although we are picking up the tab, we are not paying the ultimate price. That is being paid by the animals unfortunate enough to enter a shelter that has not embraced a culture of lifesaving. And it will not end until we put the blame directly where it belongs: *on the shelters themselves.* On the very staff and administrators who fail every time they inject an animal with an overdose of barbiturates in the face of lifesaving alternatives they simply refuse to implement.

We can—and should be—a No Kill nation today. We can save upwards of 95 percent of all impounded animals right now, if all shelters rigorously implemented the simple, common-sense programs and services of the No Kill Equation. We are not a nation of "too many animals, not enough homes"; we have become a nation of callous shelter directors who find it easier to kill than to save. The fact that it is not more common for shelters to implement the programs and services of the No Kill Equation puts the lie to the claim "No one wants to kill."

Imagine this: if every shelter did as well as communities which have embraced No Kill, we would save as many as 3.8 million of the four million dogs and cats who are scheduled to be killed in U.S. shelters this year. It is not an impossible dream. For, at the end of the day, the power to change the status quo is in our hands.

Can You Kill Your Way
to No Kill?

Part I: Death at a Midwest Humane Society

IN FEBRUARY 2007, a Las Vegas, Nevada shelter that claimed to be "No Kill" was closed down due to filthy conditions and dreadful treatment of animals. According to reports, disease was rampant and sick animals were left to die in their cages. The animals were not vaccinated on intake, healthy animals subsequently grew sick, and there was a complete breakdown of animal care. The Las Vegas shelter's story is one of incompetent leadership, a Board of Directors that failed in its oversight mandate, and a director who refused to put in place the programs and services that actually save the lives of animals. What happened in Las Vegas is a tragic example of uncaring rampant in our broken animal shelter system.

Another example of institutionalized uncaring are shelters that recklessly kill the vast majority of animals in their care in the face of responsible, proven lifesaving alternatives: in other words, run-of-the-mill high kill shelters such as those that can be found in cities and towns across America. While the mechanics are different, the underlying dynamic is the same: both kinds of shelters are outdated relics that refuse to innovate. The Las Vegas shelter's "No Kill" claim is irrelevant. In the final analysis, it had more in common with high kill shelters, and the leadership and staff who run them.

Conditions at the Las Vegas animal shelter—rampant disease, filth, neglect, and animal suffering—does not represent the No Kill movement. No Kill does not mean poor care, hostile and abusive treatment, and warehousing animals without the intentional killing. It means modernizing shelter operations so that animals are well cared for and kept moving efficiently and effectively through the shelter and into homes. The No Kill movement puts action behind the words of every shelter's mission statement: "All life is precious." No Kill is about valuing animals, which means not only saving their lives but also giving them good quality care. It means vaccination on intake, nutritious food, daily socialization and exercise, fresh clean water, medical care, and a system that finds loving, new homes.

At the open admission No Kill shelter I oversaw, the average length of stay for animals was eight days, we had a return rate of less than two percent, we reduced the disease rate by 90 percent from the prior administration, we reduced the killing rate by 75 percent, no animal ever celebrated an anniversary in the facility, and we saved 93 percent of all impounded animals. In short, from 2001 to 2004, we brought sheltering into the 21st century.

PERSONAL AGENDAS

But some seized upon the Las Vegas fiasco to promote their own agenda of defending an antiquated model of sheltering based on archaic notions of "adoptability," regressive practices, and the premise that animal life is cheap and expendable. They use the Las Vegas shelter to denounce the No Kill paradigm by intimating—sometimes directly, more often indirectly—that the Las Vegas example is the natural outcome of trying to end the killing of savable dogs and cats in shelters today.

This is a misrepresentation of the worst kind. Even the Humane Society of the United States, one of the chief architects of the paradigm of killing, called conditions at the shelter "one of the worst it has ever seen." It was extreme even in the eyes of an agency that accepts staggering high levels of killing and poor care as the norm.

By denigrating the movement to end shelter killing as akin to warehousing and abuse, and by ignoring the protocols of shelters which have truly achieved No Kill, these naysayers embrace a nation of shelters grounded in killing—a defeatist mentality, inherently unethical and antithetical to animal welfare. To imply that No Kill means warehousing, therefore, is a cynicism which has only one purpose: to defend those who fail to save lives from public criticism and public accountability by painting a picture of the alternative as even darker.

At the Las Vegas shelter, the director refused to provide basic care, failed to clean and disinfect, allowed animals to languish with illnesses and injuries, and failed to implement policies and procedures that vastly increase adoptions. This is not No Kill. This is animal cruelty. In the end, HSUS sent a team to oversee the killing of roughly 1,000 animals. The Las Vegas shelter is now killing dogs and cats after only 72 hours and officials there claim they act upon the recommendation of the HSUS team. This not only replaces one "evil" with another; it even violates HSUS' own longstanding recommendation that shelters should hold animals for at least five days.

But for those who argue that Las Vegas should be viewed as a cautionary tale against No Kill, what do they recommend instead? For two veterinarians who have made a career out of opposing the No Kill philosophy, the answer is simple and is found at the local shelter in which they work.

LIFE AND DEATH
AT A MIDWEST HUMANE SOCIETY

In 2007, over a period of several weeks, 73 cats were taken, one by one, off of the adoption floor of a Midwest humane society, to a room outside of public view. One by one, each was injected with poison from a bottle marked "fatal-plus." One by one, their bodies went limp and slumped to the table. One by one, each was put to death. Why were these 73 cats killed?

They were killed, according to published reports, because the shelter decided to keep every other cage empty and curtail other lifesaving
programs, reducing the number of adoption cages by half. But since cats
occupied those cages or were under the "care" of those other programs,
they needed to be killed first. According to the Orwellian logic of shelter
bureaucrats, killing cats by cutting the capacity of the shelter in half
would allow the shelter to save more cats overall.

At this shelter, every other cage was kept empty even though disease
can be reduced by isolating sick animals, vaccination, proper handling,
good cleaning and disinfection protocols, and reducing animal stress
through daily interaction and socialization by volunteers. At the same
time that the number of cages was reduced by half, the shelter also re-
stricted adoption hours and eviscerated its foster care program.

In response to a public backlash, the architect of this policy claimed:
"I am not in any way advocating for more euthanasia," which is more
double-speak as this is exactly what is being advocated. What else is the
option when the number of cages is reduced by half while the shelter cur-
tails other opportunities to save them?

Her argument was also lost on a reporter who noted that, in fact, killing more cats and cutting shelter capacity in half means more cats die, a
fact confirmed by the rising death toll for cats in the shelter. Before the
veterinarian who instituted the new policies started working there, the cat
death rate was on a multi-year decline culminating at about 20 percent.
Since she started with the shelter in 2003, the death toll for cats has risen
steadily. It has been increasing every year since. Even while the Society
is getting wealthier (its annual revenue is growing by the millions), it is
killing more cats than in recent history, despite falling intakes.

According to an exposé published in the local weekly:

> The [kill] rate has not gone down. The shelter still kills about
> one-third of the nearly 7,000 animals it receives annually. And
> the numbers for cats are the worst. The shelter is actually taking in
> fewer felines—3,000 so far this year, compared to 3,800 in 2006—
> but is killing more of them. In 2003, the Humane Society [killed]
> 600 cats a year. By 2006, it was killing more than 1,200. And it's on
> track to kill an even higher number this year.

On top of this, the humane society's new rules:

> Decreed that old or sick cats—even those with treatable con-
> ditions—would be [automatically killed]. Kittens that arrive needing
> to be bottle fed would also generally be killed, since the Humane
> Society limited the number of foster families available to care for
> them to just 10.

This approach is contrary to the No Kill Equation, the only model
that has actually succeeded at creating a No Kill community. By contrast, traditional sheltering policies that say shelters can keep half the
cages empty, kill neonatals rather than send them into foster care, turn
away the volunteer foster parents who come forward to help, and restrict
adoption hours are little more than a tool to legitimize the "adopt some
and kill the rest" approach to sheltering of the last 150 years.

In short, the model advocated by the Midwest humane society is a resounding failure. What its shelter managers, veterinarians, and consul-
tants call a "counterintuitive" policy is actually a contradiction. More cats
are being killed because that is what happens when you kill more cats!
More cats are killed because when you intentionally keep half the cages empty and you do not offer alternatives to killing, you kill more cats!
More cats are killed because some, like neonatal kittens, need foster care
and when you limit foster care, you end up killing more cats! More cats
are being killed because you limit the number of adoptions when you cut
back the days you are open for adoption.

As progressive shelters have demonstrated, disease can be reduced
by vaccination, increasing adoptions, sending animals to foster care,
using volunteers to socialize the animals, careful handling, and thorough
cleaning and disinfection protocols.

This has not been lost on the cat-loving public. According to volunteers, respiratory infections had nothing to do with keeping the cages
full. They were the result of shelter staff "ignoring basic protocols, like
washing their hands between handling animals."*

---

* The shelter's director did ultimately admit to a reporter that the shelter has never had
an epidemic of a serious disease, further undermining the claim that these new policies
were needed.

REJECTING THE STATUS QUO

While some shelters and their regressive allies continue to dig trenches to the past, the rest of us are building bridges to our inevitable No Kill future. In doing so, we reject the consensus of killing and reject the "model" that says killing is inevitable because the animals do not meet draconian and myopic definitions of beauty or satisfy regressive and obsolete notions of "adoptability."

In the end, our movement is about more than compelling shelters to simply label themselves as "No Kill" and proceed with business as usual, as the Las Vegas shelter did. Our movement is about action and results, not mere words and promises. What we seek is a modernization and transformation of our shelters: we demand that they exchange century-old, obsolete forms of doing business that recklessly embrace killing as a morally defensible means to an end, with policies that uphold the life and welfare of animals as paramount and direct operations accordingly.

What we demand, and what the animals deserve, are shelter directors and veterinarians who value life and keep pace with progress and innovation, including the new and comprehensive animal shelter protocols developed over the last decade to keep animals healthy and well cared for, while finding homes for *all* those who are savable.

But those who have seized on the Las Vegas fiasco do not. Why?

THE SEMMELWEIS REFLEX

Historians have coined the term the "Semmelweis Reflex" to describe "mob behavior in which a discovery of important scientific fact is punished rather than rewarded." In the 19th century, Dr. Ignac Semmelweis observed a higher incidence of deaths due to puerperal fever in maternity wards associated with teaching hospitals than in births attended by midwives. In trying to figure out why puerperal fever was a hazard of giving birth when assisted by a doctor rather than a midwife, Dr. Semmelweis hypothesized that students and doctors might be carrying the diseases from autopsies they performed, while midwives—who performed no such procedures—were not. Semmelweis found that rigorous instrument cleaning and hand washing could bring the fever rate near zero. Had

doctors known at the time that germs caused disease, this finding would
have been unremarkable.

Unfortunately, Semmelweis' discovery predated the germ theory of
disease. At the time, no one knew that asepsis was important. According
to Semmelweis' critics, hand washing wasn't needed when they could
clearly see that their hands had nothing on them. And, tragically, they ignored his recommendations and continued with business as usual, with
deadly results for their patients. Once germ theory was established, however, Semmelweis' foresight was vindicated. Of course, maintaining ste-
rility through instrument cleaning and hand washing is now the norm.

The housing, socialization, adoption, foster care, cleaning and vaccination protocols, medical and behavior care and rehabilitation, and
other efforts pioneered in communities like San Francisco and cop-
ied elsewhere provide high quality care and reduce disease rates, while
keeping cages and kennels full and finding loving new homes for the vast
majority of shelter animals. These models were developed by compassionate individuals, professionals, and in conjunction with esteemed
veterinary institutions.

Rather than attack Semmelweis, doctors should have simply washed
their hands, since Semmelweis pointed out that this nearly eliminated
deaths, even though at the time no one could explain why. Likewise,
rather than attack the model of sheltering that saves the vast majority of
animals, shelter administrators should copy its precepts because it has
been shown to work in other communities. But the vast majority of shelter directors refuse.

Tragically, something more nefarious was at work in Semmelweis'
time than only a failure of understanding about germs, and the same
"reflex" is at work in sheltering today. Semmelweis was fired because
doctors felt he was criticizing the superiority of doctor-assisted births
over midwife-assisted births, something that threatened their position
in the social hierarchy. And there's the rub. The archaic voices of tradition in sheltering are acting as did the doctors who valued their reputa-
tions more than their patients. They refuse to innovate and modernize
precisely because they are threatened by the No Kill philosophy and what
this means for their own stature in the humane movement.

Part II: Life at a Northeast SPCA

When I left the San Francisco SPCA to work at Tompkins County, New
York's open admission animal control shelter, I found an organization
typical of animal shelters nationwide. There was poor quality care, disease was common, medical treatment was spotty, and too many animals
were being killed. If cages became full, the remainder was killed. If a dog
didn't get adopted right away, the dog was killed. If a cat sneezed and did
not respond to treatment within four days, the cat was killed.

I did not travel nearly 3,000 miles to continue the status quo. I resolved that despite animal control contracts that required us to keep the
doors open to the influx of new animals, I would not kill those already in
our care. The trade-off, take in one and kill another, was unethical. No
animal would be killed unless the animal was hopelessly ill or injured and
the prognosis for recovery was poor or grave. No dog would be killed for
behavior problems unless the dog was truly vicious with a poor prognosis
for rehabilitation. And no feral cat would be killed simply for being feral.
We were taking killing *off* the table. But we did not—as the Las Vegas shelter's incompetent director, staff, and Board did—simply allow animals to
languish, get sick, and die on their own.

Instead, I put the "exit" strategy in place: adoptions, marketing, foster care, pet retention programs, Trap-Neuter-Release, spay/neuter, and
more. And when it came to keeping animals healthy and treating already
sick ones, I did what any responsible shelter director would do, and what
proved to be the animals' salvation time-and-time again: I turned to the
community for help.

Accordingly, I approached the Cornell College of Veterinary Medicine.
My request to them was to create vaccination, cleaning, and treatment
protocols that would allow us to keep every cat cage and dog kennel occupied, doubling up if necessary, and also treat sick animals who would
have been killed outright prior to my arrival. I wanted to increase the
number of lives saved, while decreasing disease rates, rates of animals
dying in kennel, and animal stress levels, even as I ran the shelter at
"capacity-plus" if needed. I told them killing as a management tool was
unacceptable. When presented with the opportunity to create a life-

affirming model that took killing off of the table, the veterinary team at Cornell accepted the challenge, and the results were dramatic.

Working with a committee made up of one private veterinarian in the community with experience in shelter medicine, a staff member from the Cornell Feline Health Center, a veterinary epidemiologist from the college faculty, and the staff and faculty of the Companion Animal Hospital at Cornell University, my administration created a sheltering model that, between 2001 and 2004, reduced killing by 75 percent, reduced the return rate for adopted animals to negligible levels, reduced the number of animals dying in kennel by 90 percent, reduced both the frequency and severity of illness, and reduced length of stay to an average of eight days. (We achieved similar results for dogs with behavior problems and aggression working in concert with the Department of Behavior Medicine at Cornell.) At the same time, adoptions, foster care, rescue transfers, and lifesaving reached all-time highs.

We brought accountability and results to an "industry" that did not historically value these because there was a built in excuse ("too many animals, not enough homes") and a built in scapegoat (the "irresponsible public") that allowed shelter directors to avoid them. Because of these blame-shifting excuses, shelters have lost sight of their mission. The fundamental mission of a humane society is to save lives. Everything a shelter does should be a means to stop killing. But too many shelter directors and shelter veterinarians have forgotten this core principle; killing has simply become one more tool in the "medicine cabinet" of these managers. It sits beside the vaccinations, the parvocides, and the antibiotics. But all those other things are tools to keep animals alive. Shelters should vaccinate, clean, disinfect, socialize, foster, and implement all those other programs so they don't have to kill animals. Everything they are claiming to try to achieve is a means to the end of not killing. And so while vaccinations, parvocides, and antibiotics help us reach the goal of not killing, killing—by its very act—does not. It is an inherent contradiction to use "killing" as a means to "not killing." When you reduce programs like foster care or the number of cages to house animals that would preclude killing, you don't get closer to the goal; you move further away. If we could kill our way out of this problem, we would have been a No Kill nation many generations ago.

The response by those who cling to these outdated ideologies will be immediately obvious because it provides their rationale for the Midwest humane society fiasco: 'You have to kill some to save the majority of others.' But there are many reasons to reject this. First, this is a logical absurdity and inherently unethical. A humane society's mission is to protect animals, not to kill them when they are not suffering. Second, the rationale is false. Before officials started at this humane society, the agency was saving 80 percent of all impounded cats. For five years, it has increased the number and percentage of cats killed, despite falling cat impounds as a direct result of scaling back lifesaving programs. Five years of data is powerful proof that their view is simply wrong. Third, this is merely a variant of the century-old "adopt some and kill the rest" approach to sheltering, wrapped in the language of veterinary medicine to give it undeserved scientific credibility. Fourth, the rationale assumes that there are too many animals to save them all; a notion progressive, dedicated shelters directors nationwide have proven is utterly false.

But at the end of the day, only results matter. Do the animals live or die? And here, there can be no debate. The approach of shelters such as the humane society in the Midwest has failed—miserably. And too many cats have been needlessly killed as a tragic result.

As a movement and as a nation, we have a choice. We can embrace the No Kill philosophy, and end the unnecessary killing of millions of dogs and cats each year. Or we can adopt the model that will perpetuate it, the same model that caused 73 cats at a Midwest humane society to be killed for one reason and one reason only: They happened to enter a shelter run by a director who believed that traditional sheltering "experts" had something to teach her.

Fear Mongering at the Humane Society of the United States

NEARLY 150 YEARS AGO, Henry Bergh started North America's first incorporated humane society, the American Society for the Prevention of Cruelty to Animals. While early humane efforts primarily focused on protecting animals who had been forced into labor (e.g., horse-pulled railways), Bergh and his SPCA soon set their sights on the abuses of local dog catchers. The other SPCAs, humane societies and animal welfare groups that began to dot the American landscape, though distinct and independent, nevertheless modeled themselves after Bergh's ASPCA. While local pounds killed animals—claiming that they were a public health and safety threat—humane groups fought to save them. In other words, while animal control claims to protect *people* from the perceived threats caused by *animals*, animal welfare groups are—or should be—striving to protect *animals* from *people*. These have always been two very distinct movements, opposing each other on fundamental issues of life and death.

While we can try to bring these opposing principles closer, the tension can never be eliminated. In the No Kill philosophy, we reconcile them as much as possible, forcing accountability onto animal control so that the only animals killed are those who are hopelessly ill or injured, irremediably suffering, or in the case of dogs, truly vicious with a poor or grave prognosis for rehabilitation. But for 95 percent of the animals who do not fit these definitions, not only does the No Kill philosophy demand that shelters save them, but through the No Kill Equation, it provides the key to do so.

Only through the No Kill philosophy can we address the conflicting aims of "animal control" and "animal welfare" in a way that saves the vast majority of animals, and still protects the public from the truly vicious dog. That doesn't mean that there aren't some irreconcilable differences. There are. But we have put our cards on the table so that we can make decisions in a fair, open manner.

When we simply ignore the distinctions (pretending to ourselves and to the American public that no conflict exists) or when we profess one thing while doing the opposite, we are dishonest. At the very least, we misrepresent ourselves, hiding behind the veneer of "animal welfare" or "animal protection," when we really promote a philosophy that puts animals last or worse—even allows them to be executed based on impermissible criteria.

This problem is at the heart of what is wrong with the Humane Society of the United States. HSUS claims that it is devoted to saving dogs and cats, to promoting the bonds between people and animals, and to leading the cause of protecting them and increasing their status in society. However, such claims cannot be reconciled with their support for the killing of healthy dogs and cats in shelters to this very day.

As to why they insist on taking positions that are, at their core, inherently antithetical to animal welfare, we must look to the "actors" who compose their leadership, particularly the Companion Animal division. Here, the term "actor" is deliberate. Because while they play the public persona of animal lovers, HSUS leadership often comes from animal control organizations that kill animals, and these individuals carry that mindset to HSUS, even though it claims a *different* mission. And so they denigrate the animals they are supposed to protect, and use HSUS to veil their reactionary animal control agendas under the cloak of "animal welfare."

Until recently, HSUS' agenda of killing has dominated the national discussion of companion animals that it was essentially the only voice until the No Kill movement called it into question. In fact, the lack of challenge to this position has convinced many animal activists to accept the extreme Orwellian notion that killing is kindness, because this position comes under the mantle of large, national animal welfare groups. They have been taught to believe that animal control based on killing poses no contradiction with an animal welfare mission.

And as long as groups like HSUS ignore the distinction and bring animal control mindsets to animal welfare without a bridging philosophy that is ethical and rigorous, animal control based on killing will continue to ride roughshod over animal welfare—and compassion will fall victim to control.

DEMONIZING CATS

We can see this contradiction within HSUS when we look at their long, sordid history relating to cats. Despite progressive, proven lifesaving alternatives, and until only very recently, HSUS has called the mass slaughter of feral cats in shelters the only "practical and humane solution." HSUS asked a criminal prosecutor to conclude that programs to sterilize and release feral cats back to their habitats violate state anti-cruelty laws and subject their caretakers to arrest and prosecution. HSUS also spread hysteria about cats and bird flu, even as the World Health Organization found no risk. Over the years, HSUS has further accused cats of:

- Being a public rabies threat: "Cats are now the most common domestic vectors of rabies";
- Decimating wildlife: "Free-roaming cats kill millions of wild animals each year";
- Being invasive, non-native intruders: "Cats are not a part of natural ecosystems, and their predation causes unnecessary suffering and death;" and,
- Causing neighborhood strife: "They also cause conflicts among neighbors."

HSUS instructed shelters to denigrate cats by having them "document public health problems that relate to cats. Include diseases that are spread from cat to cat as well as those spread between cats and other animals," without regard for true risk analysis. And HSUS continues to legitimize the shelter killing of healthy and treatable cats as a "necessity."

DEMONIZING DOGS

Nor has HSUS been a model of ethical advocacy on behalf of dogs. As it does for cats, HSUS continues to view and promote the killing of dogs in shelters as necessary and proper, despite successful No Kill alternatives, and even if the animals are healthy or treatable. But fear mongering at HSUS has taken a new turn with the publication of an article in their *Animal Sheltering* magazine entitled: "*I Chose a Child's Face Over My Dog.*" The article was written at a time when No Kill proponents and "Pit Bull" advocates were gaining ground in their effort to overcome stereotypes of dog aggression and dog breeds. Tragically, the article fails to illuminate the truth about aggression or dangerous dogs, and in fact, only heightens stereotypes and perpetuates myths. That the "expert" killed his dog because of what he considered severe aggression is not what one takes from the article. That would have been a very different piece, a tragedy for all involved.

Instead, the article assumes the worst in dogs, and the worst in people who want to see fewer dogs killed. Opposition is dismissed as irresponsible. Dog lovers are pitted against children. It is the type of either-or, you-are-with-us-or-against-us, your-dog-or-your-child hysteria most of us, especially those of us who love both our dogs and our children, dismissed long ago. According to the article:

- Killing dogs becomes unacceptable only when people inappropriately "humaniz[e] dogs";
- "Millions of people are bitten by dogs every year, many tens of thousands of children";
- If you do not believe in killing dogs, you have made them "quasi-religious objects of veneration";
- "Millions of Americans seek medical attention every year for animal bites or attacks";

- "[F]or every troubled or aggressive animal kept alive for months or years, healthy and adoptable animals go wanting for homes and often lose their lives";
- "Insurance companies are paying out billions of dollars to people bitten by dogs"; and,
- Adopting a Pit Bull appears to be more trouble than it is worth.

Every one of these conclusions is deeply flawed and deeply offensive.

THE EPIDEMIC THAT
WASN'T THERE

Contrary to HSUS' claim that there is an epidemic of dog bites in the United States, the vast majority of dogs are in fact friendly and will never act aggressively toward people. If we take shelter dogs as a representative sampling of dogs in society, upwards of 97 percent are friendly to people. If we assume for the sake of argument that dogs in shelters have a higher risk of aggression due to broken bonds, less training, more time spent isolated outdoors, or having received less care than dogs who do not enter shelters, then the situation is even less worrisome. Consequently, the fear-based hysteria of dangerous dogs becomes demonstrably false.

So where did the notion of an American dog bite epidemic come from? The numbers are simply flawed extrapolations from two outdated government studies which took poorly formulated and overly restrictive samples of the population (one reported six dog bites, the other 38) and then simply multiplied those numbers by how many people live in the United States. In short, it is an extrapolation of six dog bites!

In spite of this, some groups are calling for a ban on specific breeds; others claim we need to enforce responsible animal care; others seek more and tougher laws. But these positions are not justified by the facts. There is little in the way of evidence that more regulation, more laws, and further crackdowns on dogs is justified as a way to prevent dog bites. At the end of the day, the vast majority of dogs are friendly and will never act aggressively; dogs are already heavily regulated; and there is little need for further public policy initiatives such as legislation. HSUS should stop focusing on fear-based advocacy, stop perpetuating myths, and start advocating for the dogs they theoretically exist to protect.

Despite an explosion in the number of dogs in the United States and their greater integration in society, the number of fatal dog attacks has remained relatively constant for decades. Nonetheless, dogs remain heavily regulated: they must be licensed with local authorities, they cannot go in public places without a leash (if at all), they must be vaccinated against rabies, you can't live with more than a small number of them, animal control officers can seize and destroy them if they judge a dog a nuisance, and the arbitrary and low threshold of making a determination of "dangerousness" (and thus, extermination) puts dogs at a disadvantage, even when the facts show otherwise. Together, license laws, leash laws, vaccination laws, pet limit laws, nuisance laws, health codes, property laws, and dangerous dog laws, leave little justification to tighten the noose even further.

We will never eliminate risk in society. We can minimize it, but in the case of dogs, little more can—or should—be done. And, in many ways, we need to undo some of the laws and regulations like breed bans because they allow friendly dogs to be killed without making anyone safer.

And although we are told in the HSUS article that, "Millions of Americans seek medical attention every year for animal bites or attacks," what they don't say is that over 92 percent of dog bites result in no injuries. And of those that do result in injury, 7.5 percent are minor. In fact, they are less severe than *any other* class of injury. In actuality, less than 1/10th of 1 percent (0.08 percent to be exact) of all bites rank at *moderate* or above, and in the vast majority of cases, the dog was provoked.

Even if HSUS is correct that 4.7 million people are bitten by dogs each year (they are not), over 4.66 million people have nothing to really show for it and only 0.0002 percent result in death. You are five times more likely to be killed by lightning and four times more likely to be killed by a forklift, even though very few people have contact with forklifts. I am not downplaying the death or maiming of even one single person. But creating public policy—and shelter standards—requires thoughtful deliberation, not incendiary fanaticism that reduces the discussion to meaningless debate about the value of dogs versus children, and thereby creates a less compassionate, less gentle society for all of us.

Instead of leading us to a more ethical future, HSUS fear mongering stands the HSUS mission on its head. Rather than advocate on behalf of dogs (and cats), HSUS fans the flames of misinformation that leads to their killing. That the nation's largest companion animal protection group is a leading voice of misinformation about cats and dogs, which contributes to restricting their further integration in society and needlessly losing their lives is not only a failure of leadership. It is outrageous.

Because when we argue in extremes (the child or the dog), when we demonize people who think we kill too much (dogs are "quasi-religious objects of veneration"), when we pretend to be motivated by animal welfare yet profess the beliefs of a system of killing, we do a disservice to ourselves, our children, and our dogs. And while HSUS may claim that "for every troubled or aggressive animal kept alive for months or years, healthy and adoptable animals go wanting for homes and often lose their lives," the truth once again is more sobering. "Healthy and adoptable animals" are killed in shelters because of regressive policies that allow shelters to do so. And as long as we do not challenge that as a society, dogs will continue to needlessly lose their lives.

The Fallacy of "Fates Worse Than Death"

RECENTLY, I RECEIVED a letter from a woman who has spent half a century doing animal rescue work. Her description of the experiences she has had over the years, including the heartbreaking rescue of a near-dead kitten abandoned by a dumpster, demonstrates that she cares deeply about animals. And yet, she opposes the No Kill philosophy because she believes that "there are fates worse than death." And she cannot conceive of a No Kill nation because she sees a crisis of uncaring in the United States, a conclusion drawn from decades of seeing abandoned, neglected, and abused animals. She knows this, she says, not from "percentages, data, and studies," but from "what she has seen with her own eyes."

Sadly, she and other animal rescuers who share these views have been in the trenches of rescue work so long, that they have become myopic; consequently, they have concluded that the lives of animals are filled with little more than pain and suffering. They believe in the inevitability of certain outcomes, and what they witness seems to confirm this point of view. In addition, the large national animal protection organizations which they turn to for guidance reaffirm their beliefs: people don't care, irresponsibility is rampant, there are too many unwanted animals, and the only choices for most of these animals are a quick death in a shelter or suffering on the streets. Because they lack experience at progressive shelters that would challenge these views and they have trained themselves not to see evidence to the contrary all around them, they believe that "killing is kindness" and the alternative is worse.

What is driving these misplaced perceptions is a lack of perspective—perspective which comes from a larger view they cannot see and which the animal protection movement has failed to provide. If they took a step back, if they allowed themselves to see what is happening nationally, if they kept an open mind and stayed informed about the successes of the No Kill movement, they would see something else entirely. They would see the "big picture"—which reveals that there is not an epidemic of un-caring in the population-at-large, but in fact, quite the opposite. That there is a way out of killing and that a No Kill nation is not only possible, it is happening in communities all over the United States and it is well within our reach on a national scale.

Roughly eight million dogs and cats enter shelters every year, a small fraction compared to the 165 million in people's homes. Of those enter-ing shelters, only four percent are seized because of cruelty and neglect. Some people surrender their animals because they are irresponsible, but others do so because they have nowhere else to turn—a person dies, they lose their job, their home is foreclosed. In theory, that is why shelters exist—to be a safety net for animals whose caretakers no longer can or want to care for them. And the majority of animals who enter these shel-ters can, and should, be saved.

Imagine if shelters provided good care, comfort, and plenty of affec-tion to the animals during their stay at these way stations funded through tax and philanthropic dollars by a dog- and cat-loving culture. And imag-ine if all shelters embraced the No Kill philosophy and the programs and services which make it possible. We would be a No Kill nation today.

Already, there are many No Kill cities and counties. Several of these communities doubled adoptions and cut killing by over 75 percent—and it did not take them five years to do so. They did it virtually overnight. But what happened in these places is not happening in most communities. Not because it isn't possible, but because it has not been a priority for shelter managers and bureaucrats. In these shelters, unmotivated and uncaring employees shirk their duties: they fail to feed the dogs and cats; make them sick by cutting corners on cleaning protocols; leave them in squalor; and show open hostility to volunteers who could help by socializing, grooming, and giving the animals the love and attention they deserve. These shelters refuse to make adoptions a priority, choosing to kill the animals out of expediency.

Tragically, many animals experience neglect or abuse for the first time *after* they enter shelters. The sick and fearful animals rescuers often see are the victims of the *shelter's* abuse. They see new animals coming in and the old ones leaving in body bags. And they blame the public, although the shelters refuse to implement simple, common-sense alternatives to killing. What they don't see, unless they live in a community whose shelter has embraced a culture of caring and lifesaving is a shelter filled with adopters, volunteers, well-cared-for animals, feral cats at sterilization clinics, puppies and kittens at offsite adoptions, clean cages, and kind, welcoming staff.

The contrast between a regressive, kill shelter and a fully functioning No Kill shelter could not be starker. But because they don't see the latter and have been repeatedly told that the former is the "best we can do," they ignore plainly inhumane treatment and accept a system of sheltering that is nothing short of medieval. If they had a larger perspective—a progressively run, lifesaving shelter to compare to the one they are familiar with—they would see that the tragedy is actually the nation's sheltering system, run by uncaring directors, civil-service and union protected shirkers, and politicians who have abdicated their fiduciary duty to ensure that these institutions mirror the public's values, which are, in reality, incredibly humane.

The sad fact is that our perceptions do not always reflect the truth because we can misconstrue what we experience. For instance, I recently met a veterinarian who was convinced that feral cats are suffering horribly. I explained that after twenty years of feral cat advocacy and work in the animal sheltering field, I found little evidence to support such an assertion and that, in fact, several studies reveal that they are by and large happy and healthy and enjoy a good quality of life. I asked if her perception might be obscured: Since she does not participate in feral cat spay/neuter clinics, she sees only sick or injured feral cats and never encounters the vast majority, who are thriving. "I never thought of that," she said, leaving me with the hope that I had planted a seed that would blossom into a new, more positive, and more accurate perspective.

Many in the humane movement suffer from a similarly limited perspective because of the work they do and where and how they spend their time. The problem appears larger and more pervasive than it is. Visiting poorly performing shelters on a regular basis, they lose sight of a broader, more accurate perspective of how most people really feel about animals.

They fail to realize that there are more people who care than do not care and that most people are decent to animals, concerned about their welfare, and can be trusted with their guardianship. They ignore that people spend $48 billion every year on their animals, a number that grows even as most other economic sectors are plummeting. They ignore that people miss work when their pets get sick. They ignore that people cut back their own needs during difficult economic times because they can't bear to cut back on the needs of their animal companions. And they don't recognize that No Kill success throughout the country is a result of people—*people who care deeply.*

People who volunteer at the shelter, who foster needy animals, who donate money even in times of economic uncertainty, who adopt from the shelter because their shelter welcomes them—by being clean, encouraging volunteerism, asking them to foster, treating them politely, and making it easy for them to adopt. Communities where shelters have boldly and sincerely proclaimed their desire to become No Kill have found an eager public ready to help make it a reality.

In fact, evidence of caring is often all around those who believe that others don't care enough about animals, but they can't recognize it as such or dismiss it as the "exception." Though they constantly encounter "exceptions," they don't assimilate what it means. They fail to reach the proper conclusions even when the people who adopt the animals they rescue send letters and photographs, and thank them repeatedly for enriching their lives. They fail to recognize this when they see people at the dog park, or crossing their paths on their morning dog walks around the neighborhood. They even fail to recognize them in the stories, the care, and the embraces at their own veterinarian's office—the waiting rooms never devoid of people, the faces of scared people wondering what ails their animal companions, and the tears as they emerge from the exam rooms after saying good-bye for the last time.

They don't see that books about animals who have touched people's lives are not only written in ever-increasing numbers but are best sellers because people do care, and the stories touch them profoundly. They don't see that the success of movies about animals is also a reflection of the love people have for them.

They fail to see how people were terrified as news spread of the pet food recall in 2007, when tainted pet food from China made their companion animals sick. And while animals were killed by tainted food, they were not the only ones to get hurt. Their caretakers suffered too: thousands of caring, helpless people witnessed the anguish of their pets because their government and a government overseas betrayed them for industry profits.

If they would only open their eyes, these animal rescuers would see that shelters that have fully embraced the public and implemented the necessary lifesaving programs, have proved that there is enough of this love and compassion in every community to achieve No Kill despite the irresponsibility of the few.

If those who rescue animals but remain opposed to No Kill took genuine stock of what was around them, they would see that while any case of an individual animal suffering abuse or neglect at the hands of a human is unacceptable and tragic, the number of these incidents is small compared to the number of dogs and cats loved, pampered, and cared for by the American public. To therefore use the plight of a tragic few to legitimize and endorse the systematic killing of millions by our nation's corrupt and broken animal shelter system is not merely misguided; it is egregious. And it institutionalizes abuse and neglect by failing to challenge the actual causes of the horrible situation they encounter in regressive shelters. Ultimately, by supporting these shelters, albeit naïvely, they grant absolution to those truly responsible for animal suffering and killing, and help perpetuate these tragic outcomes. In short, they make things worse by failing to demand better, and by failing to support those who are.

Ironically, though they see themselves as loving and caring, their hearts are closed. Blinded by dogma, they filter everything they see and everything they experience through the belief that animals are victims of uncaring and cruel people—*and their belief that it is a problem of such scope and magnitude that the only way out is killing*. As a result, they condone a real problem—mass killing—as a "solution" to a phantom one.

What makes this point of view especially disturbing is the illogical leap it causes people to make from a false assumption (animals are suffering in overwhelming numbers) to a violent conclusion: mass killing is acceptable, indeed desirable. Because even if the first assumption were true (it is not), the conclusion simply does not follow. There are many, many possibilities in between to combat it—education, adoption, redemption, sanctuary, rescue, rehabilitation—that are ignored simply because the notion that killing is the "logical" outcome has dominated the sheltering dialogue for so long and so completely. It is regarded as acceptable and inevitable even though it is the most unnecessary, extreme, and inhumane of all responses.

Even if a case could be made that the public does not care, embracing death for these animals remains a *non-sequitur*. While these rescuers work to stop animals from suffering, they inadvertently champion the same attitude towards them that allows for such abuse—indeed, that perpetuates it: the idea that animals do not matter, that their lives are of little value and are easily expendable. Their assumption that animals must be killed in shelters undermines the entire principle which should be motivating their rescue efforts. Animal cruelty is horrible not only because of the pain and suffering of animals but because it often kills them. And killing animals is the ultimate betrayal. To "rescue" them from abuse and potential killing only to advocate for killing makes no sense whatsoever. Even if they are not convinced of the viability of No Kill alternatives, to be responsible advocates, they are nonetheless obligated to try, especially since it works in many communities.

In the end, their argument comes down to the belief that there are fates worse than death. And, sadly, too many people in rescue work accept this notion, even though it is patently false, and incorrectly assumes only three choices are available: killing at the pound, killing at the hands of abusers, or being killed on the streets. Working hard to end the scourge of abuse and neglect—and to punish the abusers—is not mutually exclusive with saving the lives of the innocent victims. In fact, the moral imperative to do one goes hand in hand with the other.

Yet in rescue work, some argue that death for the animals is a way out of suffering, forgetting that the right to live is inviolate. These people ignore that what they seek for animals they would never seek for themselves or other people. They ignore that no matter what the context and all through history—in Cambodia, Germany, under the Taliban, in Serbia-Croatia, in Rwanda, as in Darfur—despite the savagery, people cling to life, they cling to hope, and none of the survivors (and none of their rescuers) would suggest they should have been "humanely euthanized" by their liberators. To suggest such would perpetuate the violence and abuse.

While cruelty and suffering are abhorrent, while cruelty and suffering are painful, while cruelty and suffering should be condemned and rooted out, there is nothing worse than death, because death is final. An animal subjected to pain and suffering can be rescued. An animal subjected to savage cruelty can even become a therapy dog, bringing comfort to cancer patients, as the dog fighting case against football player Michael Vick shows. There is still hope, but death is hope's total antithesis. It is the eclipse of hope because they never wake up, ever. It is the worst of the worst—a fact each and every one of us would recognize if we were the ones being threatened with death. And it is an arrogant abuse of our power over defenseless animals to think it is our right to make such a determination for them.

I am not naïve. I understand that the *method* of killing is important, and if we lived in a two dimensional world of shadows—if we lived in Plato's cave—where the choice truly was nothing more than to be killed inhumanely or to be killed in a less brutal way, we would pick the latter. Although I have called repeatedly for the end of shelter killing, I have also supported efforts to abolish cruel methods of doing so—which too many shelters have refused to do. But that is not the choice presented. The choice is not, as rescuers contend, a choice between continued suffering and death at the pound. This is not what the animals face. Once they are rescued from abuse, more suffering should no longer be an option.

No one argues that shelters should leave animals to their abusers or that we adopt animals out to them. Everyone agrees that abuse is terrible, something no animal should endure. Of course, they must be rescued from these horrible fates. But once rescued and taken into protective custody, the question becomes: Do we give them a second chance and find them homes? Or, do we allow them to become victims yet again by killing them? Why the leap to arguing that because they experienced abuse in the past, they should be killed now? Or that all the other animals entering shelters should be killed? It is patently illogical.

In essence, champions of the "fates worse than death" argument advocate a "solution" of the mass killing of millions of animals as a response to the abuse or neglect suffered by some animals, which does absolutely nothing to erase the abuse that has already been done. How is killing some animals a prescriptive against future abuse, when we cannot know nor predict when or where it is about to occur, unless we exterminate all animals, everywhere, to guard against the possibility of it ever occurring again? Taken to its logical conclusion, it would mean killing every dog and cat in every shelter. This is not only an obvious obscenity; it is to propose a slaughter with no end.

Yet despite these disturbing and misguided views, I do not believe that such people are necessarily beyond rehabilitation. Certainly, I do not legitimize their point of view, nor do I believe that future generations will look back kindly on their support of killing, even in light of their false perceptions. Ultimately, it does not matter to the dog or cat being injected with poison by a shelter worker whether the motivation is lack of caring, laziness, cowardice, politics, or a real belief in the need to do so. The consequences are the same—death—and equally tragic, irrespective of who is doing the killing and why it is being done. Yet even though they are absolutely wrong, we should not give up trying to rehabilitate them, because, in the end, they can become allies.

What they need is perspective—a larger view they cannot see from the trenches about the incredible success all around them: That the four million killed in shelters do not tell the full story. That the story is also about the *165 million* dogs and cats in homes. That the kitten abandoned in a dumpster is overshadowed—though no less tragic for it—by the great lengths people go to when their animals are sick or by the compassion of those who inevitably come forward to give that kitten a second chance. That while the shelter in their community is killing at an astonishing pace, shelters in other communities have stopped when they embraced, rather than condemned, the larger public, and committed themselves to ending the killing by asking the public for help.

It is incumbent on No Kill advocates to help them see the bigger, more accurate, and more optimistic picture. Because unlike the lazy shelter manager or the uncaring shirker or the self-serving politician, these people care about animals and can change in earnest. They can become *believers*. And when they do, they become a further force for change. We must continue to expose the fallacy of their beliefs—that the choice is between an expedient shelter death or slow suffering on the streets or in the hands of abusers; that in order to be No Kill, shelters must warehouse animals because there are too many for the too few available homes; and that, even if those were the choices, it is acceptable for activists who claim to speak on behalf of animals to accept or champion for those animals that which neither they, nor the animals if they could speak, would accept: death.

And so we come back to the primary principle of the humane movement: Animal shelters must be the safety net, not an extension of the neglect and abuse animals face elsewhere. And like other service agencies that deal with human irresponsibility, shelters should not use that as an excuse to negate their own responsibility to put in place necessary programs and services to respond humanely, and therefore, appropriately.

This is the perspective they need. And with enough of it, they'll eventually see. Eventually, they, too, will be liberated from pessimism and share in the optimism, the hope, and the tremendous potential this truth offers our animal friends. They'll have their epiphany when they finally see through the fog under which they have lived: the condemnation of the public that has been ringing out so deafeningly for decades that is has drowned out the truth and legitimized the killing. It may take some time—time and perspective—but it is our solemn duty as No Kill advocates to give it to them until they do, even while we vociferously oppose the deadly policies they currently champion.

Intentionally Lost: Animal Activists Who Embrace Death

In the prior essay, I wrote about animal activists who are lost in the fog of their own myopia. They have rejected No Kill even as it provides a way out of the suffering they see around them. They have concluded that some fates are worse than death and have accepted the falsehood that for most animals, the only choices are a quick death at the pound, or slow suffering on the streets. I argued that these activists need a larger perspective to help them see beyond the false dichotomies they have come to believe and which can turn them into allies in the fight for a No Kill nation. Though they are Naysayers, they are not beyond our reach.

But there is another kind of Naysayer in communities across the country who is beyond rehabilitation. These Naysayers aren't lost in the fog of misinformation, they are intentionally and, unfortunately, irretrievably lost. And to overcome their opposition to saving lives, we must expose them for who and what they really are.

My work in sheltering takes me all over the country, providing assistance to shelters that want to save more lives; and when they don't, to local activists and rescue groups who are working to reform them. Tragically, every community has at least one, but more commonly a small number of individuals, who oppose shelter reform. I refer to these people as "Naysayers." Although they publicly wear the mantle of the animal lover, they vehemently oppose No Kill and any effort to reform animal control, no matter how dysfunctional the department or how cruel local practices are.

Because they sometimes belong to spay/neuter organizations or "Friends of the Shelter" groups, and because they are often politically active (testifying at city council meetings for more funding for animal control, for spay/neuter, for legislation), they are perceived as "animal activists." Consequently, their opposition to No Kill and shelter reform sows seeds of doubt where none should be among local politicians and the media.

Because they exist in every community, their pervasiveness and predictability suggest shared psychological profiles. If we can better understand what motivates such individuals, we can hinder, if not eliminate, their destructive power and influence.

What identifies these Naysayers is that they ignore history, facts, and truth. They are champions of continued killing, defenders of draconian animal shelters, and purveyors of punishment through misguided legislative efforts such as pet limit laws, leash laws, and feeding bans, even when community after community has shown that such efforts kill animals.

In my book *Redemption*, I wrote:

> While some activists simply do not know better and mean well, others obstinately ignore facts, experience, and history and continue to push these types of laws. They will do what they have always done—facts, logic, and history be damned. They will continue to blame the public and they will continue to fight for more and tougher laws. They will argue that their community is different, that their situation is unique, that citizens in their community are particularly—or peculiarly—irresponsible. None of this is true, but they do not care.
>
> While they claim to be motivated by saving lives, there is something much more powerful driving them: *the desire to punish*.

An activist truly focused on lifesaving, who subsequently learns
that punitive legislation is not only a dismal failure, but that it
has the opposite results (more impounds, more killing), would
end their support of such methods and begin to push for regime
change at animal control or the programs and services of the No
Kill Equation. By contrast, those who are intent on punishing the
public are being driven by other imperatives. In the end, they so
want to punish the public for not taking care of their pets as much
as they think they should, they are willing to ignore all the evidence
about legislation's true results or about how to truly save lives, and
instead empower animal control to kill animals in the process. Unfortunately, animal control is generally more than willing to oblige
and do just that. In the end, these activists become that which they
claim to most despise—people whose actions result in the impound
and killing of animals. *They* become the "irresponsible public."

Clearly, these individuals are not motivated by saving animals: they
spend no effort on shelter reform or shelter reform legislation; they refuse to acknowledge that problems exist in their local shelter in spite of
the overwhelming evidence that proves it; and they don't stop to consider
that their punitive laws send animals to horrible and abusive pounds—
which they often defend.

In fact, they stand side-by-side with the perpetrators in speeches and
legislative hearings. And while No Kill advocates believe in spay/neuter,
encourage spay/neuter, and promote incentives for spay/neuter, many
oppose the mandatory spay/neuter laws they champion. That is neither
a contradiction nor a philosophical position. If these laws worked, true
No Kill advocates would be their first and loudest champions. Instead, we
understand that if one is goal oriented, and if the goal is reducing shelter
intakes and shelter deaths, support for mandatory spay/neuter laws does
not necessarily follow the belief in the importance of spay/neuter.

Over and over, legislation is pushed as a quick solution to high rates
of shelter killing. "If only we had a law," the argument goes, "all the bad,
irresponsible people would have to take care of their pets properly, and
shelters wouldn't have to kill so many animals." If this were true, given the
proliferation of punitive mandates nationwide, these laws would create

many No Kill communities. That there are none as a result of punitive legislation proves that such legislation is far from a cure-all. In fact, it often has the opposite effect. Communities that have passed such laws are not only far from No Kill; many are moving in the opposite direction.

Mandatory and punitive laws are largely a distraction. Studies show that people who do not spay/neuter are at the lowest rungs of the economic ladder. And that the vast majority would spay/neuter if it was free. Increasing the numbers of animals who would be in violation of a new law while failing to write "no impound" and "free" or "subsidized" spay/neuter into the law, increases the number of animals in violation and subject to citation and/or impound. Because the pounds make no effort to build the infrastructure to save those lives once they enter, more animals are killed.

Unfortunately, Naysayers nationwide have internalized the viewpoint that the public, *rather than the shelter*, is to blame for the volume of killing. Since the very "solution" they propose makes the goal impossible, however, they seek more citations, greater penalties, more animals subject to impounding, and more draconian laws, broadening the divide between the shelter and the public, and moving further and further from true lifesaving with each piece of punitive legislation.

Their promotion of punitive legislation diverts focus from establishing vital programs such as offsite adoptions, non-lethal feral cat programs, and foster care in favor of traditional enforcement: more power for animal control departments, more officers, more sweeps of animals, more citations written, more animals impounded, and more animals killed. (They also feed the backyard breeder market as people then acquire other unaltered animals.) That individuals who claim to be concerned with high levels of shelter killing actually seek legislation to empower their dysfunctional animal control bureaucracy to impound—and kill— even more animals, is conveniently ignored.

In 2008, while California mandatory spay/neuter proponents attended a legislative hearing with shelter directors whose facilities were infamous for poor, hostile, and even abusive care of animals, a senator asked one of the proposed law's chief proponents: "This bill doesn't even pretend to be about saving animals, does it?" In a moment of candor, the shelter director responded: "No, Senator, this is not about saving dogs and cats." For shelter directors, it is about increasing the power of animal control. It is about getting more money for enforcement. It is about diverting focus from their own failures to save lives by getting activists who might challenge them to focus on a straw man: the "common enemy." It is about control, not compassion.

For the Naysayers, it is about establishing their superiority to the uncaring masses, whose rule is threatened by the emerging success of the No Kill movement, which proves that while *some* people are irresponsible, *most* people do care. Most people find killing abhorrent. Most people pass on their own needs during difficult economic times to provide what their animals need. Most people would do the right thing if given the information they need to make good choices. Most people are not only part of the solution; they are the key to it. And that, according to these Naysayers, is unacceptable. Because if it was, these "animal advocates" aren't so "special" anymore. Most people are not only as committed to animals as they claim to be; they are more so because they oppose killing, too. And this is something they cannot accept. So they block it out, because what else do they have? Who else are they? To recognize the truth is to lose their identity as "saviors"—these addicts of being "special" at the expense of the animals.

The strategy to overcome these people is simple: Because they can never be convinced to change their point-of-view, true animal lovers working to reform their local shelters must remove any legitimacy these Naysayers have, by isolating and exposing them for who and what they really are; that they are not motivated by "saving animals." That these emperors have no clothes and that they are ugly in their nakedness—disingenuous, and misanthropic in their elitist disdain for other people and their lack of true commitment to the best interests of animals. In the end, they are nothing more than bullies. And because the only way to stop a bully is to stand up to a bully, No Kill advocates must fight back.

Sit, Fetch, Stay or Die

THEY ARE the voiceless victims of dogfighters. They are perpetually exploited by the media looking for a sensational story. Self-serving politicians pass legislation demanding their systematic destruction while wrapping themselves in the mantle of public safety. Some groups call for automatic death sentences for these dogs in shelters, while other groups promote policies that lead to killing them in various contexts. Shelters temperament test them literally to death, falsely claiming the vast majority are "unadoptable." And self-proclaimed "experts" advocate that even if they are friendly, they can't be trusted around children and other animals and thus should be killed anyway. Add poorly performing shelters who find killing easier than doing what is necessary to stop it, and the chances of Pit Bulls escaping regressive shelters alive are daunting.*

---

* There are three breeds commonly referred to as "Pit Bulls"—the American Pit Bull Terrier, the American Staffordshire Terrier, and the Staffordshire Bull Terrier. But recent research shows that shelters misidentify breeds roughly 87 percent of the time. When it comes to dogs we call "Pit Bulls," shelters are not only unnecessarily killing them based on breed stereotypes, but they are killing dogs they mistakenly think are Pit Bulls, despite being wrong about their breed in almost nine out of ten cases.

Just as often, however, those selling them out claim to be loyal advocates. They say they champion Pit Bulls—while pursuing policies that lead to their destruction. The new catchphrase in this kind of pro-Pit Bull killing apologia is "ambassador for the breed." According to a shelter with a Pit Bull ambassador program, "The goal is to debunk myths associated with the breed." The idea is to adopt out only "perfect" Pit Bulls so that when they are in the community, they can show people that the Pit Bull can be a model dog they need not fear.

Yet another shelter with a "model" Pit Bull ambassador program says that "Dogs who make it into this program undergo extensive health and temperament screenings before they are adopted out." A dog must score 100 percent on the following tests to become an "ambassador" and thus make it out of the shelter alive:

- Accept a friendly stranger;
- Sit politely for petting;
- Appearance and grooming;
- Walk on a loose leash;
- Walk through a crowd;
- Sit, down, and stay on command;
- Come when called;
- Reaction to another dog;
- Reaction to distractions; and,
- Supervised separation.

What happens to those dogs not deemed "perfect"? While some ambassador programs allow for dogs deemed imperfect to be adopted and simply withhold the label "ambassador," many shelters kill them if they do not satisfy the mandates. In other words, these shelters kill Pit Bulls who are not "perfect," even if they are friendly. In that context, the "ambassador" program creates yet another excuse to kill these dogs. And while this program is billed as a way of "debunking the myths" associated with Pit Bull-type dogs, it actually perpetuates them. It sets Pit Bulls apart from other dogs, perpetuating the idea that they are different and potentially dangerous. It perpetuates the idea that their lives matter less than other dogs, so killing them is acceptable. It sets the bar so high that it perpetuates the paradigm wherein the majority of Pit Bulls must be killed. In other words, they have to sit, stay, come when called or die—something we would never accept as a standard for other dogs in shelters. It is yet another way of blaming the victim, of blaming the killing on the dogs themselves—of peddling unfair stereotypes and accepting killing in spite of alternatives.

To protect public safety, we cannot include truly aggressive dogs in shelter adoption programs, Pit Bull or otherwise. But it is a far jump from that reality to a conclusion that dogs that pull on the leash must be killed. If in their excitement, they greet by jumping on you, they are killed. If they do not sit politely while being petted, they are killed.

In other words, the "ambassador for the breed" program does little more than provide shelters that kill the vast majority of Pit Bulls with a "seal of approval" from supposed advocacy groups. With no criteria to determine whether or not the program is changing public perception, no timetables for evaluating it, no clearly defined, quantifiable goals as to what success is, and no suggestion of when it can be expanded to Pit Bulls deemed "less than perfect," the ambassador program may delay the time when the vast majority are saved.

To be effective advocates, we must challenge—rather than sanction—ideas that institutionalize killing. Rather than start with the prevailing paradigm of killing and embrace an incremental approach by saving a few "perfect" dogs, we must start with the goal of ending their killing and embrace the programs and services that will get us there fastest. In other words, the Pit Bull ambassador program gets it backwards.

The program also ignores the fact that roughly nine out of ten Pit Bulls *already* debunk the aggression myths; most of these dogs are *not* aggressive. According to national temperament testing results, about 87 percent of owned Pit Bull-type dogs are friendly. The numbers in a shelter environment are similar. About nine out of ten Pit Bull-type dogs should pass a fair evaluation for aggression (In Tompkins County, it was 86 percent when I was the director).

Some of these dogs will obey commands, others will not. Some will eat your kid's breakfast when no one is looking, some will think all shoes are dog toys, some will dig up your garden, some will take over the bed

when you visit the bathroom at 2:00 am, some will greet you by jumping up on you with muddy paws, some will be shy, some will pull on the
leash, some will think that—though they weigh 80 pounds—they can sit
on your lap and then shift around to get more comfortable. None of these
behaviors indicate that the dogs are also aggressive. Lack of manners, ex-
citability, and love of food should not be a death sentence and, in fact, are
all normal dog behaviors. Consequently, Pit Bulls who may have these behaviors are still worthy of being saved, even if someone deems them "imperfect." And since they are not aggressive, they are already ambassadors
for the breed in showing that they are not the mean, vicious dogs that they
are made out to be.

Right now, however, the overwhelming majority of Pit Bulls who end
up in shelters are killed. And most of them are friendly. The only difference between a shelter that simply kills them and one that claims to promote ambassador programs is the seal of approval to the killing that the
latter provides. In the end, the notion undermines the foundation of the
No Kill movement that every animal who can be saved must be saved.

Our duty is to expose the myths and disproven dogmas that have allowed for the pointless slaughter of roughly two million dogs every year in
our nation's shelters, including Pit Bulls. Rather than dismantle this deadly paradigm, those proclaiming to defend the breed by promoting the "Pit
Bull Ambassador" approach actually create a new rationale for the killing of
savable animals and perhaps, worst of all, officially sanction it.

The "ambassador" approach assumes that the lives of individual
animals are not paramount. That these individuals can be sacrificed for a
perceived greater good: the lives of a few we deem "perfect." Ultimately,
it is simply repackaging "catch and kill" sheltering in a new fuzzy label:
"ambassadors for the breed."

Facts, figures, comprehensive adoption programs, and passionate,
unyielding advocacy are needed to undo the years of misinformation and
abuse by which Pit Bulls have suffered. Challenging the status quo and
exposing hypocrisy is not easy and never pleasant, but we must do so.
Gimmicks that sanction the harmful ideas we are supposed to be fighting
and sacrifice the lives we are supposed to be saving violate our core duty.

SIT, FETCH, STAY OR DIE

Our movement cannot change attitudes regarding these dogs by embracing programs that legitimize them.

Rather than embrace a program based on the deadly idea that it is acceptable to sacrifice the many to save a tiny few, how about treating them just like dogs and working to save all of them? After all, "Pit Bulls are just dogs. Four legs, two eyes, one heart." (Delise, Karen, *The Pit Bull Placebo*, Anubis Publishing, 2007.) We should treat them that way. That is what compassion and justice dictate. And that must be the first premise of our advocacy on their behalf.

The Feral Cat's Wild Life

THE HUMANE MOVEMENT makes many assumptions about feral cats, the quality of their lives, and how they should be treated. These assumptions, however, do not stand up to scrutiny. And they result in treating feral cats contrary to the principles which guide the way such groups advocate for other animals. This discrimination results in their opposition to lifesaving measures such as Trap-Neuter-Release (TNR)—or simply leaving the cats alone—and promotion of needlessly killing them instead.

These unsupportable claims include:

The myth that cats belong indoors. According to groups like the Humane Society of the United States, cats belong indoors, shelters should have "indoor-only" adoption policies, and companion animal groups should admonish people for allowing their cats to go outdoors. Yet the idea that cats belong indoors is contrary to the natural history of the species, which has flourished outdoors for over 100,000 years as a subspecies of the Wildcat, and as a so-called "domestic" animal for 10,000 years. Several studies confirm that from the cat's perspective, the great outdoors really is great. A comprehensive 11-year study of outdoor cats found that they had similar baselines in health, disease rates, and longevity as indoor cats. A subsequent study gave feral cats "A+" grades across a wide range of physical and health characteristics. In yet another study, less than one percent of over 100,000 feral cats admitted to seven major TNR programs across the United States were killed for debilitating conditions; while a fourth survey across 132 colonies in north central Florida showed that 96 percent of feral cats had a "good" or "great" quality of life.

Of course, there will always be a small percentage of cats who fall outside these norms. Rather than use this as an excuse to justify the rounding up and killing of all feral cats, we must recognize that all animals face some hardship; hardship is an unavoidable condition of life on earth. But, like all animals, feral cats also experience the joys of life. Life, by its very definition and common experience, is a mix of easy and hard, good and bad, happy and sad. We experience it as humans. Raccoons experience it, too. So do birds, fox, mice, and rabbits. But that does not lead us to conclude that these creatures should face mass slaughter. As the target of a call for mass extermination, the feral cat stands alone.

Since animal protection groups do not support the trapping and killing of other wild animals, why do they reserve this fate for feral cats? Since feral cats survive in the wild like wild animals and are unsocial to humans like wild animals, shouldn't we treat them as we do other wild animals—by advocating on their behalf, pushing for their right to life, and respecting and protecting their habitats? And why should we condemn *all* of them to death because of the sloppy logic that *some* may face hardship?

The answer from opponents of TNR programs—that we should stop cats from being killed by killing the cats ourselves is a hopeless contradiction. But the contradiction goes deeper. While traditional shelters argue that all cats are the same, they themselves hold feral cats to a deadly double standard. Once in the shelter, a "friendly" cat may be deemed suitable for adoption. An "unfriendly" cat, by contrast, is killed outright, often within minutes of arriving.

Some opponents of TNR claim that feral cat advocates are the ones with a double standard: *if feral cats are wild, why TNR? Why not leave them alone as we do other wild animals?* It is not because feral cats are suffering that No Kill proponents advocate TNR. We advocate TNR to reduce

conflicts between the cats and humans and to stop their killing in shelters.* In the absence of conflicts with people, the ideal would be to simply
leave them alone, the same ideal we hold out for other wild animals. But
because cats seek out humans the way that pigeons do, and because they
have been legally classified as "domestic," they end up in shelters where
most are killed.

Meanwhile, proponents of the "cats belong indoors" myth ignore
the fact that indoor cats face serious risks as well. As a general rule, a cat
allowed to play outdoors is friendlier, healthier, and happier. The rise in
obesity and behavior problems in cats can be linked to the move by the
humane community to indoor-only cat adoption and advocacy policies.
While it is possible to provide needed exercise and socialization to cats
confined indoors, it is worth noting that it is nice to go outside. It feels
good. It is stimulating. We want it for ourselves. We should not deny the
outdoors to our cats except where there is true risk, such as for those living in downtown Manhattan or on a very busy thoroughfare.

In the end, however, the "risks" associated with being outdoors—disease, malicious humans, and even predation—are not the primary killers
of cats. (A study on the diet of urban coyotes in an area filled with outdoor
cats showed that domestic cats were found in only 1.3 percent of the scats).
People in shelters are the number one killer of cats. If we care about cats,
we should put programs in place that prevent them from entering these facilities and that provide an opportunity for them to get out alive when they
do. And the answer to how we do this for feral cats is clear: TNR.

In fact, TNR could save the lives of social cats when they enter shelters, too. Just because they are "suitable for adoption," doesn't mean social
cats actually will be adopted. At this time in history, many shelters are little
more than assembly lines of death for cats. Right now, shelters without a
TNR program kill all—or virtually all—feral cats. Shelters also kill social cats
and kittens roughly 60 percent of the time. Given that all cats have the ability to care for themselves, No Kill advocates should demand and promote
TNR for all healthy free-roaming cats, regardless of whether they are social
or unsocial to humans, if the alternative is being taken to a shelter that will

---

* In fact, some communities have also undertaken sterilization campaigns for both deer
and pigeons, in lieu of killing, when they are perceived to clash with humans.

kill them. Ideally, free-roaming social cats should be adopted into loving homes. But it doesn't follow that until we successfully reform shelters so that they provide cats with homes instead of death, we should kill these cats. TNR for even friendly, free-roaming cats is far more ethical than killing.

The myth that people do not want feral cats around their neighborhood. Most "nuisance complaints" about cats involve reproductive behaviors such as spraying, fighting, and mating. When cats are sterilized, these behaviors usually disappear. TNR programs have been shown to reduce "nuisance" complaints by as much as 80 percent.

Ironically, because the humane movement has conditioned people to think that free-roaming neighborhood cats are "suffering," it is often cat lovers who call animal control to pick up cats, believing that the local pound will find homes for these cats. Once educated to the facts, they oppose round up and kill campaigns. A 2007 study showed that 81 percent of people believe that leaving a free-roaming cat outside is more humane than having the cat caught by animal control and killed.

The myth that if the cats cannot be released back to the original location or there is no caretaker, it is better for them to be killed in a shelter to prevent future suffering. Every day, shelters take in feral cats who have lived their entire lives outside. The vast majority of these cats are healthy despite the absence of a known caretaker. The outdoors is, after all, their natural habitat. Like raccoons, skunks, and opossums who end up in shelters when trapped and brought there, we must also release feral cats back to their habitats. The fact that we keep cats as companions in our homes does not mean they are incapable of surviving, and even thriving, on their own. The ability to adapt is a central characteristic of the species.

Take the wildest cat and he can learn to live around humans and may even exhibit petlike behavior to the person who feeds him. (This is a familiar sight at cat colonies with feral cats who rub up against the legs of their feeders.) Take the most pampered, healthy companion cat and let her loose in the wild, and she too can survive with the deftness of a wild animal. Henry David Thoreau wrote in *Walden*:

> Once I was surprised to see a cat walking along the stony shore of the pond, for they rarely wander so far from home. The surprise

was mutual. Nevertheless the most domestic cat, which has lain on a rug all her days, appears quite at home in the woods, and, by her sly and stealthy behavior, proves herself more native there than the regular inhabitants.

The myth that cats are a public health and safety risk. The facts contradict this claim. In a study of feral cats living on campus in close proximity to students, faculty, staff, and visitors, Stanford University found virtually no incidence of cat-associated diseases. After consultation with the Santa Clara County Health Department and Stanford's Department of Comparative Medicine, the study concluded that feral cats pose virtually no health and safety risk to humans.

Rabies: Roughly 1/100th of 1 percent of the total U.S. cat population is diagnosed with rabies, a percentage that constitutes a negligible risk. There has not been a case of rabies transmitted from cat to human in the United States since 1975 (over 30 years ago). Moreover, since a rabies vaccine is part of every TNR program, even this minimal risk is eliminated: there have been no known cases of cats contracting rabies if they have received at least one vaccination.

Toxoplasmosis: A study in the *British Medical Journal* found that "Contact with cats, kittens, cats' feces, or cats who hunt for food was not a risk factor for infection... No significant associations were detected between infection and presence of cats (whether adult or kittens), the diet and hunting habits of the cats, or cleaning a cat's litter tray." The study concludes that eating undercooked meat is the primary risk factor in contracting the disease.

The myth that TNR programs are expensive to implement. In fact, it is more expensive not to implement a TNR program. It is far less expensive to neuter and release a cat than to take in a cat, hold and care for the cat, kill the cat, and then dispose of the body. Neutering alone results in savings due to reduced births. Three major studies prove this. A Florida study showed that by neutering rather than impounding and killing feral cats, a local jurisdiction saved over $650,000 in a six-year period. A 10-year Ohio study found that cat impounds and deaths were increasing in shelters statewide, with the exception of the shelter with a TNR program. And an analysis of impound and death rates in San Francisco's public shelter found that field impoundments were down 65 percent, adult cat deaths were down 82 percent, and kitten deaths were down 93 percent thanks to the TNR effort, all at great cost savings to the municipality.

The myth that cats are decimating bird populations. While bird species' decline is evident, almost all reputable studies identify a different cause: *habitat destruction by humans.* Another major culprit is the use of pesticides—particularly toxic lawn care products, insecticides, fungicides, and rodenticides. Other studies point to drought, forest fragmentation, and trapping by humans. Unless we conclude that predation studies conducted on four continents are all wrong, feral cats should no longer be unfairly implicated in any decimation of bird populations.*

The myth that cats are "non-native" and therefore less important than so-called "native" animals. The idea that some animals have more value than others comes from a troubling belief that lineage determines the value of an individual animal. This belief is part of a growing and disturbing movement called "Invasion Biology." The notion that "native" species have more value than "non-native" ones finds its roots historically in Nazi Germany, where the notion of a garden with native plants was founded on nationalistic and racist ideas "cloaked in scientific jargon." This is not surprising. The types of arguments made for biological purity of people are exactly the same as those made for purity among animals and plants.

In the United States, Invasion Biologists believe that certain plants or animals should be valued more than others if they were at a particular location "first," although the exact starting point varies, is difficult to ascertain, and, in many cases, is wholly arbitrary. Indeed, all plants and animals were introduced (by wind, humans, migration, or other animals) at some point in time. But regardless of which arbitrary measure is used, Invasion Biologists ultimately make the same, unethical assertions that "introduced" or "non-native" species do not have value and are not worthy of compassion. They conclude that these species should, therefore, be eradicated in order to return an area to some vague, idyllic past.

Trying to move the world to a mythical state that probably never existed lacks a moral or logical foundation. Nature cannot be frozen in time

* For a more detailed analysis of predation studies, see *Redemption: The Myth of Pet Overpopulation & The No Kill Revolution in America*, at pp. 76-79 (2nd Edition, 2009.)

or returned to a pre-European past, nor is there a compelling reason why it should be. To claim that "native" species are somehow better than "introduced" species equally or better adapted to the environment is to deny the inevitable forces of migration and natural selection. No matter how many so-called "non-native" animals (and plants for that matter) are killed, the goal of total eradication can never be reached. As far as feral cats are concerned, they will always exist. To advocate for their eradication is to propose a massacre with no hope of success and no conceivable end. They exist and have a right to live, regardless of how and when they arrived or were "introduced." Their rights as individuals supersede our own narrow, human-centric desires, which are often based on arbitrary biases, subjective aesthetics, or commercial interests.

The ultimate goal of the environmental movement is to create a peaceful and harmonious relationship between humans and the environment. To be authentic, this goal must include respect for other species. Tragically, given its alarming embrace of Invasion Biology, the environmental movement has violated this ethic by targeting species for eradication because their existence conflicts with the world as some people would like it to be. And in championing such views, the movement paradoxically supports the use of traps, poisons, fire, and hunting, all of which cause great harm, suffering, and environmental degradation.

Equally inconsistent in the philosophy of Invasion Biology is its position—or, more accurately, lack of a coherent position—on humans. If one accepts the logic that only native plants and animals have value, human beings are the biggest non-native intruders in the United States. With over 300 million of us altering the landscape and causing virtually all of the environmental and species decimation through habitat destruction and pollution, shouldn't Invasion Biologists demand that non-native people leave the continent? Of course, non-profit organizations that advocate nativist positions would never dare say so, or donations to their causes would dry up. Instead, they engage in a great hypocrisy of doing that which they claim to abhor and blame "non-native" species for doing: preying on those who cannot defend themselves.

In the end, it is not "predation" that Invasion Biologists object to. Animals prey on other animals all the time without their complaints. In fact, they themselves prey on some birds by eating them, and they prey on animals they label "non-native" by eradicating them. For Invasion Biologists, predation is unacceptable only when it involves an animal they do not like.

It is wrong and obscene to label any species an "alien" on its own planet and to target that species for extermination. Disguised under the progressive mantle "environmentalism," this emerging field of pseudoscience would more accurately be labeled "biological xenophobia."

The myth that the goal of TNR is "no more feral cats." For many cats, their status as "domestic" animals means slaughter in a shelter. Sadly, classifying them as "wild" doesn't help. In some states, unprotected species of wildlife are subject to trapping, poisoning, and hunting. Feral cats, in essence, are caught between two anachronistic worldviews. The feral cat serves as a grim reminder of how far we have yet to go as a humane movement and as a society.

As there will always be cats and cat lovers, as cats get lost or are abandoned and join feral colonies, as cats are hardy and extremely resilient survivors, and as cats have lived side-by-side with humans for 10,000 years, feral cats will always exist in our communities. Our goal is not, and never was, "no more feral cats." Our goal is no more *killing* of feral cats. At this time in history, that can be most expeditiously accomplished through TNR, by giving them protected status under law, by outlawing their killing, by making it illegal for them to enter shelters in the first place, by expanding the concept of what constitutes their habitat to the broadest interpretation (i.e., outdoors), and through an abolition of trapping by people, shelters, governments and "pest control" companies for purposes of removing cats to be killed.

Feral cats have the right to live and the right to live in their habitats. This position is no different than our views about habitat protection for raccoons and other wildlife. They share our communities and their needs must be accommodated. After all, it's their world too.

No Movies Celebrating Dogs

JUST AS WHEN the Walt Disney company re-released *101 Dalmatians*, shelters across the country rattled their sabers when Disney recently released the film *Beverly Hills Chihuahua*. They claimed that the movie would lead to the neglect, abandonment, and death of dogs as people flock to buy Chihuahuas, tire of them, and then relegate them to shelters, where they would be killed.

People for the Ethical Treatment of Animals proclaimed that "Impulsive purchases that ensue mean that the dirty backyard-breeding market booms. Ultimately, animal shelters overflow." PETA claimed that the movie would be "a death sentence for dogs in animal shelters." In the San Francisco Bay Area, several shelters issued a joint press release claiming to be bracing themselves for the onslaught of Chihuahuas because of the movie. Outside the Bay Area, some called the movie's release "irresponsible."

In a recent article in *Newsweek*, a PETA spokesperson said she,

> still remembers the re-release of the Disney classic *101 Dalmatians* and the tragedy that followed. First there was a spike in sales of the

famous spotted breed. Then, in the months that followed, shelters took in hundreds of Dalmatians from disillusioned pet owners around the country. "As soon as the puppies outlived their cuteness and the kids didn't want to scoop the poop anymore, the dogs were dumped in shelters... Many of them had to be [killed], because there was simply no place for them to go."

But this viewpoint fails to recognize the true cause of killing in our nation's shelters. If there was a spike in Dalmatians being surrendered after *101 Dalmatians* was released, the truth is that none of them had to be killed. It is not that "there was simply no place for them to go." It is that they ultimately went to places where animals don't matter because killing is the acceptable norm. If Chihuahuas were killed in shelters, just like if Dalmatians were, it was because shelter directors ordered them to be killed, despite readily available lifesaving alternatives.

In fact, Disney promoted responsible care of dogs by stating both on the homepage of the *Beverly Hills Chihuahua* movie website and at the end of the film that dogs are a lifelong responsibility and that people should adopt rather than purchase an animal. To that end, they explicitly stated:

> Dogs require daily care and constant attention. Before bringing a dog into your family, research the specific breed to make sure [he/she] is suitable for your particular situation. Learn about and be willing to undertake the serious responsibilities of dog care. Always consider adoption from a reputable shelter or rescue program.

Even the dog in the film was rescued from death row in a killing shelter.

The sad truth is that there will always be some irresponsibility. *If* some people saw the movie and *if* they went out and got a Chihuahua, and *if* they ultimately surrendered the dog to a shelter, it does not follow that shelters needed to kill any of them. We should not be angry at the Walt Disney company. We should be angry at shelters that will use Disney as their latest in a long line of blame-shifting strategies to justify killing.

The programs and services of the No Kill Equation—programs that should be implemented regardless of *Beverly Hills Chihuahua*—would allow shelters to save these dogs and all the others. If there is a central lesson from the No Kill movement, it is that every community has enough love and compassion to overcome the irresponsibility of the few. The shelters in No Kill communities have proven that they can find loving, new homes for all the savable dogs in their facilities, despite any short- or even long-term crises that arise above and beyond normal intake. That is why death rates in some communities continue to decline significantly despite an increase in impounds as a result of the housing and economic meltdown.

Despite the consistent drum beat by groups that there are already too many animals and not enough homes—a claim which flies in the face of a thriving pet store and puppy mill industry—the fact is that every year, millions more people look to bring a new dog into their home than the total number of dogs entering shelters. Additionally, not all dogs entering shelters need adoption. When you add up those dogs who are lost strays and can be reunited with families out looking for them, those who are irremediably suffering or truly dangerous, and subtract their numbers from total impounds, the reality is that shelters have to find homes for a smaller percentage than it seems. People love dogs, want to live with dogs, and if the message is correct and the opportunities available, will adopt dogs from shelters and rescue groups.

Have we come to the point where our false dogmas about an irresponsible public and the need to kill have convinced us that we cannot even highlight dogs in movies for fear that people will want to share their lives with them? Is this really what we want—a ban on movies about dogs? "Sssh, loving dogs is a secret. Let's not talk about them, forget putting them in a book, and, rule number one, let's not show them in movies. And while we are at it, let's ban *Lassie, Old Yeller, Because of Winn Dixie, Benji, The Call of the Wild, 101 Dalmatians, Beverly Hills Chihuahua*, and all the rest of them because people might fall in love with dogs and go out and get one!"

Nonetheless, PETA and local shelters issued press releases or public statements citing all the usual platitudes about "impulse" adoptions and how irresponsible people are, saying that they are getting prepared for the onslaught of Chihuahuas. We can only shudder at what "getting ready" means for PETA, as they kill over 90 percent of animals they take to their facility and do almost no adoption outreach. But what does it mean for shelters? Are they ramping up adoption promotions? Are they building foster care networks? Are they staffing more offsite adoption locations? Are they solidifying partnerships with breed rescue groups? Are they doing anything proactive? If history is any indication, sadly, the answer is no.

The reality is that shelters should be doing all of these things anyway, and too many are not. In fact, in one shelter, staff and volunteers were fired for fostering nursing animals and bringing them back when they were old enough for adoption because the shelter director—a darling of the Humane Society of the United States—didn't want a foster care program, even though three decades of experience at progressive shelters has shown that lifesaving success is very difficult without one.

The line of thinking goes as follows: "Because people are bad, they can't be trusted with dogs, and so we have to kill them because the alternative is worse." No one is good enough. The animals are better off dead. This justifies a deadly paradox: making it incredibly easy to surrender an animal but incredibly hard to adopt one. And the same logic underlies the misguided *Beverly Hills Chihuahua* salvo by animal rights groups and animal shelters against a company that makes movies with messages that are anti-fur (*101 Dalmatians*), anti-hunting (*Bambi* and *Brother Bear*), anti-pound killing (*Lady & the Tramp*), anti-cat killing and pro-feral cat (*Aristocats*), anti-rat killing (*Ratatouille*), anti-fishing (*Finding Nemo* and *Little Mermaid*), and encourage respect for the environment (*Pocahontas*).*

Ultimately, this campaign was but another attempt by our nation's shelters to blame shelter killing on others. And because they falsely claim

---

* In fact, as one commentator pointed out ten years ago, Walt Disney himself believed in animal rights, attended a humane education conference in Chicago, and has done a tremendous amount to promote animal rights: "No one has done more to further those ideals than Disney, who in *Bambi, 101 Dalmatians,* and *Dumbo* indicted the cruelty inherent in hunting, the fur trade, and circuses… and in countless other ways redefined cultural perceptions of how humans should relate to animals." However, this isn't a full scale endorsement of the Disney corporation. In 2005, they rejected a humane group's effort to neuter and release stray friendly dogs living around the parking lot of the Hong Kong Disneyland and being cared for by construction workers. They also refused to find them homes. Instead, they had the dogs rounded up and killed by local dogcatchers in the run up to the grand opening of the amusement park.

it is beyond their control and a *fait accompli*, shelter killing ceases to be an ethical or humane issue. Hence a group can call itself, without the slightest hint of irony, People for the *Ethical* Treatment of Animals or *Humane* Society of the United States and yet unabashedly support the shelter killing of healthy and other savable animals.

In countenancing an animal control mentality that worries about saving animals but not killing them, the matriarch of this "catch and kill" philosophy, the late-Phyllis Wright of the Humane Society of the United States, said:

> I've put 70,000 dogs and cats to sleep… But I tell you one thing: I don't worry about one of those animals that were put to sleep… Being dead is not cruelty to animals.

From this point of view come the cries about "impulse" adoptions and the need to kill without the data to see if these dangers even exist. Shelters and national groups have historically railed against programs in which shelters take animals offsite, to malls and other high traffic areas, claiming this encourages impulse adoptions. And that such adoptions lead to neglect and abandonment. Thirty years of data, however, yield no factual evidence for this claim; in fact, adoptions from offsite venues are less likely to fail than those from other places. And even if it is true that people adopt from these sites on impulse, why do we always assume the worst? Indeed, humans are capable of many good and noble impulses, including adopting from a shelter and giving that animal a lifetime, loving home.

One of the shelters that issued a press release about the film goes even further, citing a dubious statistic for a dubious proposition: that 15 percent of the dogs they placed last year were Chihuahuas and the movie will inevitably drive up the percentage. But what is the relevance of this? In fact, this particular shelter actively seeks out small dogs from out of its county jurisdiction because they claim that is what the public wants and because it runs out of "adoptable" dogs within its own city. If 15 percent of its intake is the Chihuahua, it is because they go out to other counties looking for them to satisfy public demand. This does not sound like a crisis. This sounds like success. We are, after all, in the business of adoption.

Assisting and rehoming dogs is the mission of shelters. There will always be orphaned and homeless animals in need of assistance. The duty and obligation of animal shelters, therefore, is to establish effective and humane ways to handle the intake of these animals, as has been shown to be possible at shelters in communities that have rejected killing.

That groups like PETA and shelters mired in dogma anticipated killing before the movie was even released is obscene given the lifesaving success evident in other communities, and given how monumentally the predicted outcome violates the mission they exist to fulfill. The behavior is also an embarrassment and an indictment of their failed leadership and defeatist model.

This is not to say that it would be a good thing if Chihuahuas were surrendered to shelters. Broken bonds harm dogs. Going to any shelter is not necessarily a good thing for dogs. But if the dog isn't being given the love, care, attention and life he deserves, shelters can and should provide these dogs a better alternative. That doesn't mean the obscene act of killing by PETA and others. It means a loving, new home. If some people do act irresponsibly, as some people will, no Chihuahuas should or need be killed.

Instead, shelters have created such hatred and distrust of the public that they embraced the premise that our culture can never highlight dogs or make movies about dogs because people will inevitably go out and get them, neglect them, and dump them in shelters to be killed. The reality, however, is far more positive. Collectively, we share our homes with seventy-five million dogs. We talk to them, keep their pictures in our wallets, celebrate their birthdays, travel with them, and greet them upon coming home even before saying hello to the spouse and kids. We include them in holiday celebrations and take time off from work to care for them when they are sick. And when it is time to say good-bye, we grieve.

Every year, we spend more than $48,000,000,000 dollars on our animal companions (including cats and others). And we provide hundreds of millions more to charities and shelters that promise to help animals in need, with the largest of these having annual budgets in excess of one hundred million dollars. Most Americans today hold the humane treatment of companion animals as a personal value, reflected in our laws, the proliferation of organizations founded for animal protection, increased per capita spending on animal care, and great advancements in veterinary medicine.

Instead of the fear mongering based on draconian stereotypes, platitudes, and mistruths, how about a campaign to appeal to the best in our dog-loving American culture? How about building on the message of *Beverly Hills Chihuahua* about how much people love their dogs and the great lengths they go to care for them:

> CHIHUAHUAS ARE GREAT. ADOPTING ONE IS EVEN GREATER.
> If you walk out of the movie in love with Chihuahuas or dogs in general and want to add one to your family, educate yourself about proper care, common characteristics, what you can expect, and your responsibilities. Then if your family determines this type of dog is right for you and your family is right for this type of dog, please adopt one from a shelter or visit any of the number of breed rescue groups in your community.
>
> To that end, here is a list of groups and shelters which can help you find your new best friend, regardless of whether he or she is a Chihuahua or any of the other great dogs waiting for someone to fall in love with them at your community shelters and rescue groups.

Now that is a campaign I could get behind.

I could even get behind telling potential Chihuahua families that buying from pet stores fuels the puppy mill industry, a system of over-breeding, inbreeding, minimal veterinary care, poor quality of food and shelter, lack of human socialization, overcrowded cages and killing once an animal brings no more profit to the facility. I could get behind a campaign looking at where movie companies get dogs used in filming, how they are trained, where they are kept, how they are treated, and where they go when the filming ends.

I could get behind many campaigns around this issue. What I *cannot* get behind is the dire foreshadowing, and preemptive apologia for the totally unnecessary killing of Chihuahuas. I *cannot* get behind organizations that see phantoms of doom rather than opportunities to seize upon the educational and lifesaving potential created by people's love of dogs and our popular culture's reflection of that love. I *cannot* get behind shelters and national organizations unwilling to stop a kill-oriented outcome of their own creation, and which they alone have the power to prevent. We should be better than that as a movement. And one day—when the regressive leadership that currently runs shelters and national animal advocacy groups is swept aside—rest assured, *we will be.*

The Great Abortion
Non-Debate

All across the United States, feral cat groups, rescue groups, and No Kill shelters are spaying and neutering animals, with the ultimate goal of reducing shelter intakes and killing. In fact, high-volume, low-cost spay/neuter is a core program of the No Kill Equation. Spay/neuter leads to fewer animals entering the shelter system, allowing more resources to be allocated toward saving lives. Other than leaving them alone, no-cost neutering for feral cats through a program of Trap-Neuter-Release (TNR) is the key to keeping them out of shelters and reducing their numbers humanely.

The vast majority of these organizations, however, also spay pregnant females. In the process, the kittens or puppies are killed. So far, few have questioned the ethics of doing so. But that doesn't mean that as a movement we shouldn't. Those groups that have questioned it, and are uncomfortable with the practice, still defend doing so. According to the spay/neuter coordinator of one of the nation's largest rescue organizations:

Trapping a feral mama and kittens later can be a challenge. People who use our low-cost program might not bring in the mama cat again and her kittens for spay/neuter. And we know that a cat can become pregnant again while nursing.

The coordinator went on to say that even without this problem, the ethics of spaying pregnant animals is a question better suited for the future: "When we save the already born animals, spaying pregnant animals will become unethical because the kittens or puppies will be guaranteed a home."

As to the first excuse, the underpinning of the No Kill philosophy is that we would never end life when that life is not suffering, and—in light of the sanctuary and hospice care movements—even that latter principle is subject to debate. A pregnant animal should be offered sanctuary in a foster home, where she can give birth, raise and wean her litter, before she—and they—are adopted into loving homes (or, in the case of a feral mom, spayed and released back to her habitat). That is the *only* proper and ethical thing to do.

To accept the second rationalization, we have to believe that we can't save them all. But we can, given that pet overpopulation is a myth: With 17 million Americans looking for three million available shelter animals, the calculus isn't even close. Moreover, these are kittens and puppies, the most "adoptable" of animals.

We also have to believe that allowing these animals to live somehow displaces those already alive, a nexus that is tenuous, at best. In other words, the mere fact that a litter of kittens is born and homes are found does not mean an identical litter of kittens at the local shelter will be killed because of it. Such cause and effect can never be determined and, in fact, does not exist. Lack of homes is not why shelters kill puppies or kittens.

As I wrote in *Redemption*,

There are many reasons why shelters kill animals at this point in time, but pet overpopulation is not one of them. In the case of a small percentage of animals, the animals may be hopelessly sick or injured, or the dogs are so vicious that placing them would put adoptive families at risk.* Aside from this relatively small number of cases ... shelters also kill for less merciful reasons.They kill because they make the animals sick through sloppy cleaning and poor handling. They kill because they do not want to care for sick animals. They kill because they do not effectively use the Internet and the media to promote their pets. They kill because they think volunteers are more trouble than they are worth, even though those volunteers would help to eliminate the "need" for killing. They kill because they don't want a foster care program. They kill because they are only open for adoption when people are at work and families have their children in school. They kill because they discourage visitors with their poor customer service. They kill because they do not help people overcome problems that can lead to increased impounds. They kill because they refuse to work with rescue groups. They kill because they haven't embraced TNR for feral cats. They kill because they won't socialize feral kittens. They kill because they don't walk the dogs, which makes the dogs so highly stressed that they become "cage crazy." They then kill them for being "cage crazy." They kill because their shoddy tests allow them to claim the animals are "unadoptable." They kill because their draconian laws empower them to kill.

Some kill because they are steeped in a culture of defeatism, or because they are under the thumb of regressive health or police department oversight. But they still kill. They never say, "we kill because we have accepted killing in lieu of having to put in place foster care, pet retention, volunteer, TNR, public relations, and other programs." In short, they kill because they have failed to do what is necessary to stop killing.

Moreover, even while No Kill Advocates encourage spay/neuter, even while humane groups promote it, even while high-volume, low-cost spay/neuter is a central tenet of the No Kill Equation, this effort is a *means* to an end. It is not the goal itself. The goal is *not* "no more animals

---

* This killing is also being challenged by sanctuaries and hospice care groups, a movement that is also growing in scale and scope and which all compassionate people must embrace.

being born." The goal is, and has always been, "no more animals being killed" (or, in the case of puppy mills, abused). Killing animals to prevent killing is not only a logical absurdity, it is patently unethical.

No matter what rationale is used to justify the killing, it can never be reconciled with the No Kill philosophy. In fact, proponents of "catch and kill" sheltering use "practical" arguments in favor of ending life all the time, such as "Killing dogs and cats is necessary because there are too many animals and not enough homes" or "Feral cats suffer on the streets and therefore killing is the compassionate option." These are all arguments based on a calculus of life and death, the number of homes and the number of animals in shelters, and potential suffering. While such arguments are easy to dismiss because the calculus is all wrong, they are nonetheless arguments that advance *expediency*, over what is the *right*— and therefore, moral—thing to do.

Philosophically, advancing a practical over an ethical argument has long been the safe haven for those who want to justify untoward practices. Even accepting the sincerity of the claim, even if the practical calculus was correct, saving life that is not suffering is a timeless and absolute principle upon which responsible animal advocates must tailor their practices. *Every* action they take must be subservient to preserving life. More often, however, the practical calculus is wrong and at least historically, has been used to excuse atrocities.*

Indeed, the underpinning of the No Kill movement is that it goes beyond what is commonly assumed to be a practical necessity. It is, first and foremost, a movement of beliefs, of morality and ethics, of what our vision of compassion is now and for the future. Our success is a result of

---

* For example, revisionist historians claim that, "Thomas Jefferson had slaves because he was a victim of his own time." Many of Jefferson's contemporaries, however, refused to participate in slavery on ethical grounds. But Jefferson did, even as his words on the Declaration of Independence clearly illustrate he knew better. Even if everyone owned slaves and abolitionist viewpoints did not exist, however, the notion that owning slaves is wrong could be morally deduced from our shared human experience. So we should not excuse Jefferson's conduct. Likewise, as No Kill advocates, we should obviously know and do better than condone the killing of unborn puppies and kittens based on "practical" arguments. Ethics will always trump the practical and the two are seldom so inexorably linked that an untoward action must follow some fixed practical imperative.

our philosophy dictating our actions and thereby prompting us to do better; to embrace more progressive, life-affirming methods of sheltering.
Before many of us felt comfortable with the answer to questions of whether or not feral cats suffered on the street and whether or not No Kill was
possible, we had already rejected mass killing. We had rejected practical
explanations based on a "too many animals, not enough homes" calculus,
or that a humane death was preferable to potential future suffering. Early
in our advocacy, even if we did not know the practical alternative to killing in shelters, we knew that killing was wrong and we rejected it.

No Kill is, at its core, about the rights of, and responsibilities we have
to *individual* animals. This tenet is summarized by one of the Guiding
Principles of the *U.S. No Kill Declaration*:

> Every animal in a shelter receives individual consideration,
> regardless of how many animals a shelter takes in, or whether such
> animals are healthy, underaged, elderly, sick, injured, traumatized,
> or feral.

But are No Kill and feral cat advocates living up to this principle?
Our attitudes and practices regarding pregnant animals reveal a glaring
contradiction. When we spay pregnant animals and the unborn kittens
and puppies die, the fact that they are not yet born does not relieve our
responsibility toward assuring their right to live. When we abort kittens
and puppies, we are literally killing puppies and kittens.

If the kittens or puppies are viable, they must be individually killed,
usually through an injection of sodium pentobarbital. Even when they are
not, however, when a mother is spayed, the kittens or puppies die from
anoxia (oxygen deprivation) due to lack of blood supply from the uterus
once the vessels are clamped. They suffocate.

The hope is that they would be under anesthesia, just like the mother, so they would not be "aware." However, since they are more resistant
to anoxia than adults, they could theoretically start to recover from the
anesthesia before they died. Granted, the recovery may last only a second
or two; perhaps even a fraction of a second. Or it might not happen at all.
But in the end, it does not really matter. Once dead, no one is *aware* of being dead—that is true by definition and is not the reason the act of killing

is unethical. Killing robs an individual of their life, regardless of whether or not they are able to conceive of it beforehand. It is a violation of their most basic right.

In addition, unlike the human context, the issue is not clouded by cases of rape or incest, and there is no question about the mother's choice because a dog or cat cannot consent. Literally speaking, we are trapping a mother against her will, cutting her open, and killing her offspring, and we claim to do so for her and their own good.

For a movement founded on the rights of the individual, ending the lives of unborn puppies and kittens is indefensible. Indeed, the more widespread No Kill becomes, the more we will find significant ethical dilemmas within our own practices and beliefs. Dilemmas that will challenge some of our deeply held convictions, which we may find—if we address them honestly—are still rooted in traditional apologia: killing for space, killing to prevent possible future suffering, killing as a population management tool: the unethical practices we thought we rejected when we challenged the status quo with our No Kill ideals. We have certainly come a long way as a movement, but we still have a long way to go.

Our Movement's
"Underground Railroad"

A RECENT FEATURE in St. Paul, Minnesota's daily newspaper highlighted the transport of death row dogs from communities in the South into Minnesota. The transport is part of a nationwide network of animal lovers who save dogs in high kill rate jurisdictions and take them to shelters, rescue groups, and even loving, new homes in states where the demand for dogs is said to outstrip supply. It has been compared to the "Underground Railroad" before and during the antebellum period, when slaves were smuggled out of Southern States and transported North and ultimately to Canada to gain their freedom.

I have always supported transport programs. As director of Tompkins County's animal control shelter, and as a No Kill community, we imported animals from killing shelters outside our jurisdiction rather than allow the cages to sit empty during off-peak periods. We also worked with out-of-county breed-specific rescue groups and No Kill organizations to transport some of our animals.

When exporting animals, we never sent them to killing organizations, or to shelters where local animals were killed to make room for ours. In fact, I always asked the rescue groups we worked with why they didn't just take animals from their own community shelters. Some were very breed-specific and had greater capacity than supply. Others had tried to work with their own shelters, but were rebuffed.

In terms of impounding animals into Tompkins, there was one crucial difference between our county and Minnesota. Tompkins County is a No Kill community. The communities served by Minnesota's largest shelter are not. In fact, the shelter kills over 40 percent of dogs, but it is one of those importing dogs from the South. Isn't the killing of Minnesota dogs to import dogs from places like Kentucky and Oklahoma ethically dubious? Some people and some groups have taken the position that it is. And this point-of-view has some appeal.

In the immediate aftermath of Hurricane Katrina, the Humane Society of the United States sent displaced dogs to kill shelters nationwide, instead of using some of the tens of millions of dollars they raised for Katrina rescue to find the animals loving new homes themselves. These dogs displaced local dogs who were killed to make room for the new arrivals. Katrina dogs, for example, were sent to animal control in Los Angeles, where shelters are little more than assembly lines of death. I visited a kill shelter in the Midwest that was housing Katrina dogs. Because the dogs were globally undersocialized and traumatized, they were being held for an extended period of time for rehabilitation. At the same time, however, they were killing local dogs "for space." How are these cases an ethically acceptable trade off?

As the nation's largest and wealthiest animal protection group which claims millions of members and has a national (indeed, global) reach, HSUS could have saved the dogs themselves. Instead, HSUS shipped them out to kill shelters as quickly as possible, closed up shop, and left the area with millions of dollars raised for Hurricane Katrina rescue efforts as yet unspent.

But the issue is more complicated when rescue groups are involved because they lack HSUS' capacity and therefore have not developed the infrastructure to house the animals while they are trying to find homes. And with their own shelters doing nothing to assist and continuously threatening to kill animals, they are compelled to transport the animals quickly. In No Kill communities where the demand for dogs truly does outstrip supply, it is a non-issue and a welcome effort. It is also a non-issue and welcome effort when breed rescue groups in other states are involved and capacity once again exceeds local supply. But, even beyond these, we may be missing the bigger picture when we ask if transferring animals from killing jurisdictions to other killing jurisdictions is ethical—without considering the context of transports.

If shelter managers were passionate about saving lives and implemented the programs and services that make it possible, there would be little debate about high-volume transports. They would make sense, as some parts of the country are more populated and naturally have a higher demand for animals. And if local governments were committed to a high level of service in animal care and sheltering, again, there would be little debate about transports. Everyone would support it, though the need would not be so great. It would simply become what it should be: part of a flexible strategy dedicated to saving the lives of animals.

There is nothing so unique about the South that precludes No Kill success. In fact, some of the most successful communities, with the highest rates of lifesaving, are in the South, including communities in Kentucky, Virginia, and elsewhere. The Charlottesville SPCA, which runs the animal control shelter for the City of Charlottesville and Albemarle County, has been No Kill for three years. But many shelters in these communities have made no effort to try. In 2007, for example, when I visited an animal control shelter in Louisiana, it had *only one cat available for adoption* despite killing 92 percent of them. Instead, it maintained an inordinate number of empty cages, which allowed staff to socialize amongst themselves, rather than work. The animals had no chance. Since the director was removed and a new director was hired, live releases have increased 245 percent.

At the same time, some draconian killing shelters are in the North. The problem of shelter killing is neither geographical, nor somehow "cultural," as some have suggested. The source of the problem is more pedestrian: rampant uncaring and incompetence at shelters across the country; and equally rampant uncaring and incompetence by the department bureaucrats and elected officials charged with overseeing them.

The reality is that too many shelters in too many communities are not doing their jobs. Consequently, they are unnecessarily killing a large number of animals. In addition, it is never entirely cut and dried whether one particular rescue dog will result in the killing of another (local) dog. When the transported dogs face certain death because they are in the hands of shelter managers who aren't interested in saving them, it would be wrong to say they shouldn't be saved by transport. Our first duty is to the dogs who face certain death today. There can be no blame, therefore, for the rescue groups in high kill rate jurisdictions that are sending these dogs across the country.

While they are working to save dogs by transport, however, they and others should be working equally hard to reform their local shelters or those shelters will be killing or threatening to kill dogs in perpetuity. As long as animals are regarded by shelter managers and elected officials in places like Sallisaw, Oklahoma—where the "shelter" is little more than a desk, a manager, a couple of cages, and a room to kill animals—as cheap and expendable; and as long as rescuers ship them elsewhere, there is no incentive to change. That doesn't mean the transports should stop. They shouldn't. An animal's life is not a bargaining chip. But it is painfully ironic that the medieval shelter in Sallisaw, with its regressive policies and antiquated conditions, has a higher save rate than shelters in Minnesota, to where the dogs are being shipped, precisely because the dogs are being shipped elsewhere. Tragically, some rescuers in the South see the problem as inevitable—and not, therefore, what it *really* is: the fault of officials in places like Sallisaw. The problem is *not* inevitable; it can be fixed.

Likewise, in many ways, it is also not the fault of the rescue groups taking in these dogs. There are plenty of homes available, and shelters in Minnesota should be able to save local dogs and dogs from the South. Minnesota has roughly two percent of the U.S. human population. As a percentage of the population, based on national figures, roughly 150,000 Minnesotans will look to get a dog each year, and there are roughly 30,000 dogs being killed in the state. If 80 percent of those people got a dog from somewhere other than a shelter, shelters should still zero out deaths.

From a larger No Kill perspective, however, Minnesota rescue groups should be saving dogs from their own communities. Taking the long view, if they focused on creating a No Kill community, they would save dogs beyond their borders by increasing the pressure for neighboring

communities to do the same. The old environmental slogan of the 1970s—
think globally, act locally—is apt. San Francisco's success in the mid-1990s
was the catalyst for the entire No Kill movement. Tompkins County's
success a few years later forced surrounding communities to reevaluate
leadership and practices and aspire to more lifesaving. It also ended the
fiction that animal control could not be No Kill, and therefore increased
the pressure on other animal control shelters to do the same.

Once one community achieves No Kill, people in surrounding communities begin to ask the question: "If they can do it there, why can't we
do it here?" And the pressure to do so begins to mount. But the long view
is difficult to reconcile with dogs facing mass extermination today.

Moreover, the reality is that in some parts of Minnesota, regressive
shelter management makes acting locally difficult. According to local
rescuers, some shelters won't proactively reach out to them when they
are preparing to kill dogs. Instead, leadership at these facilities appears
content to mislead the public into thinking that no savable dogs are being killed in its shelters. Therefore, they operate under a cloak of secrecy
that costs dogs their lives. In addition, even if they did not import these
other dogs, it is not clear they would save more local dogs. Long standing complaints about many empty cages at these shelters while dogs are
killed suggests otherwise.

But this much is clear: If Minnesota shelters worked more proactively with rescue groups, if they were more comprehensive with adoption
efforts, if they focused harder on reclaiming lost dogs, if they put into place
all the programs of the No Kill Equation, they could save roughly 95 percent
of the dogs they take in—and save dogs from places like Oklahoma. But they
don't. Instead, they hide behind their own mediocrity, saying that though
they kill 42 percent of dogs, it is "better" than the national average.

There are many problems with this claim. Based on dog bite extrapolation data and the results of the best performing shelters in the country,
we know that over 90 percent of dogs are savable. The most successful
communities in the country save between 91 percent and 97 percent of
dogs, so their claim that they have no choice but to import dogs from outside the state because there aren't any "adoptable" dogs locally to meet
adoption demand is patently false. With a 42 percent rate of killing, they
are killing many, many dogs who can be saved.

In addition, the national average for killing dogs is now less than 35 percent. They are not doing *better* than the average—they are doing *worse*. Moreover, why should an organization aspire to be average? Is mediocrity the goal of shelter leadership? Shouldn't they instead seek to be the best—to save 95 percent of all dogs? By that comparison, they are doing miserably. Finally, the killing is unnecessary, wrong, and the antithesis of their mission. To admit to killing 42 percent—indeed to boast of it as an achievement when so much more is actually possible—is to admit to failure.

So what is the solution? How can dogs be saved both in the South in places like Sallisaw, and in Northern communities like those in Minnesota? What ended the need for the "Underground Railroad" was the elimination of the problem: the elimination of slavery. While No Kill advocates work to save the victims of a broken animal shelter system, they must also replace their broken system with one equal to the task with which it has been entrusted.

If Minnesotans demanded and received passionate leadership committed to saving lives, they could have it all. They could save local dogs. They could also help dogs in places like Kentucky and Oklahoma. If animal lovers did the same in places like Sallisaw, they, too, could have it all. There would be less pressure to transport every dog possible North because they'd be saved at home. At the same time, they could transport dogs out of their state to their heart's content, without displacing dogs in some receiving communities. In the end, the answer to both problems, and to all the previous questions, is two-fold: *Regime change in the leadership of shelters across the country*. And *shelter reform legislation* that removes the discretion shelter managers have to needlessly kill animals. We need to regulate shelters the same way we regulate other agencies that hold—and in this case, abuse—their power over life and death.

Sadly, because of built in excuses like pet overpopulation, the irresponsible public, and the economy; because of weak leadership on the issue from the large, influential national animal protection organizations; because of underperformance at shelters and rampant uncaring in government bureaucracies, that may be easier said than done. But while these interests may be entrenched, they are not insurmountable. It is a battle we are capable of winning—and will ultimately win. And the sooner we do so, the quicker we can end this needless killing.

Good Homes Need
Not Apply

I'VE DEVOTED the last 17 years of my life to reforming animal shelters in the United States (far longer doing rescue). I've worked at two shelters that have the highest rates of lifesaving in the nation: one as its Director of Operations and the other as the Executive Director. I've also worked and consulted with dozens of shelters nationwide. Currently, I run the national No Kill Advocacy Center, which is dedicated to ending the systematic killing of animals in shelters.

In my work to reform antiquated shelter practices, I often face traditional sheltering dogma that is a roadblock to lifesaving innovation. Too many shelters operate under false assumptions that cause animals to be killed. If shelter directors reevaluated, rather than hid behind conventional wisdom, they would more be more successful at saving lives.

One of the most enduring of these traditional dogmas is that animal shelters must kill because the public cannot be trusted with animals. I faced this attitude when I arrived as the new Executive Director of the Tompkins County SPCA in upstate New York. Other than prohibiting killing, I had planned to quietly observe the agency for the first couple of days on the job: I wanted a sense of how the agency was run. An elderly gentleman and his wife came in as I was standing behind the counter observing our adoption process. After looking at the animals for some time, they came to the front counter to adopt a cat. The man told the adoption counselor how he adopted a cat from us 15 years ago. "She died one year ago today," he said. As much as they missed having a cat, he explained, he and his wife waited one year to get a new cat because they wanted to mourn her appropriately. As he told the story, he began to cry and walked away. His wife explained that her husband loved their cat very much, but they were indeed ready to love another one. Because they found a great cat here 15 years ago, they came back to us.

They filled out the application: *Do they consider the adoption a lifetime commitment?* Yes. *Do they have a veterinarian?* Yes. *What happened to their other cat?* Died of cancer. "In my arms," the old man said. But one thing caught the adoption counselor's eye. When they came to the question asking about where the cat would live, they had checked the box: "Mostly indoors, some outdoors."

"Sorry," the adoption counselor said. "We have a strict indoor-only rule." She denied the adoption. They were stunned. *I* was stunned.

What happened to "15 years," "in my arms," "wanted to mourn her appropriately," "lifetime commitment"? I overruled the counselor and gave them the cat. No fees, no more paperwork: "Let's go get your kitty," I said. I put her in their carrier and told them we'd see them in another 15 years. They thanked me and left.

I looked at the adoption counselor and told her: "We've got to take a more thoughtful approach to adoptions."

She stared at me blankly.

"Ok," I said, "Let me put it this way. Outdoor cats may face risks, but it largely depends on circumstances. We need to use common sense. This isn't downtown Manhattan. This is a rural community. I only saw one car on my way to work this morning. In fact, given how safe it is, people should be *required* to let the cat go outside." I smiled.

Nothing.

So I continued: "Outdoor cats may face risks, but so do indoor cats. They are just different ones and we don't always see the causal connections, such as obesity and boredom. Fat and bored cats are at risk for diabetes, heart problems, and even behavior problems." Still nothing. My then shelter manager stepped in and said that they were following the policies of the Humane Society of the United States. And HSUS says that people—and therefore shelter adoption policies—must keep cats indoors.

Over forty years ago, the late Phyllis Wright of HSUS, the matriarch of today's killing paradigm, wrote in *HSUS News*,

> I've put 70,000 dogs and cats to sleep... But I tell you one thing: I don't worry about one of those animals that were put to sleep... Being dead is not cruelty to animals.

She then described how she *does* worry about the animals she found homes for. From that disturbing view, HSUS coined a maxim that says we should worry about saving lives but *not* about ending them and success-fully propagated this viewpoint to shelters across the country. For many agencies, the HSUS standard is the gold standard. It is not uncommon for shelters to state they are "run in line with HSUS policies." Consequently, it's very easy to surrender an animal to a shelter and very hard to adopt one because of a distrust of the public. And after turning away adopters, these shelters often turn around and kill the same animals.

In reality, most people care deeply about animals and can be trusted with them. Evidence of this love of animals is all around us: we spend $48 billion a year on our companions, dog parks are filled with people, vet-erinary medicine is thriving, and books and movies about animals are all blockbusters because the stories touch people very deeply. Nonetheless, HSUS blames the public and because it has significant influence over shelter policies, promotes this view through shelter assessments, national conferences, and local advocacy. Consequently, it has failed to educate shelters to take more responsibility for the animals entrusted to their care. As a result, HSUS has impeded innovation and modernization in shelters. The result: unregulated, regressive shelters slavishly follow-ing the protocols of HSUS based on an idea that no one can be trusted. The employee at Tompkins County's SPCA embodied this attitude. Such people are not *really* worried about the remote possibility that the ad-opted cat would one day get hit by a car and killed; they kill cats every day—obviously, killing is not the concern. Instead, staff at the Tompkins

County SPCA at that time—like many shelters—can simply say they are operating "by the book," even though that meant unnecessarily killing animals every year in the process. In other words, I came face to face with mindless bureaucracy.

I challenged the Tompkins County SPCA shelter manager on this score, asking her how it made sense to kill cats today in order to save them from *possibly* being killed at some time in the future. "HSUS says," she responded, "that in order to increase the number of adoptions, we have to reduce the quality of homes"—we must, as a staff member of HSUS once later quipped, basically "adopt Pit Bulls to dog fighters." And that, she stated, is something we should not do.

Tragically, this is a commonly held misperception in the culture of animal sheltering, but the facts prove otherwise. Increasing adoptions means offsite adoption events, public access hours, marketing and greater visibility in the community, working with rescue groups, competing with pet stores and puppy mills, adoption incentives, a good public image, and thoughtful but not bureaucratic screening. It has nothing to do with lowering quality. It has *absolutely* nothing to do with putting animals in harm's way. Indeed, shelter killing is *the* leading cause of death for healthy dogs and cats in the United States. Adoptions take animals *out* of harm's way.

Moreover, successful high-volume adoption shelters have proved that the idea that one must reduce *quality* of homes in order to increase *quantity* is merely the anachronism of old-guard, "catch and kill" shelters that must justify high kill rates and low adoptions. Quality and quantity are not, and have never been, mutually exclusive. As one progressive shelter noted:

> The best adoption programs are designed to ensure that each animal is placed with a responsible person, one prepared to make a lifelong commitment, and to avoid the kinds of problems that may have caused the animal to be brought to the shelter.

I agree. I have long been a proponent of adoption screening because I, too, want animals to get good homes. But truth be told, in shelters where animals are being killed by the thousands, I'd rather they do "open adoptions" (little to no screening) because I trust the general public far more than those who run many animal control shelters—those who have become complacent about killing and willfully refuse to implement common-sense lifesaving alternatives. In fact, I recently assessed a municipal shelter with poor care and a high kill rate in one of the largest cities in the country. They practice open adoptions and volunteers have long clamored for adoption screening. My recommendation was as follows:

> This is an area where volunteers have repeatedly suggested some form of screening to make sure animals are not just going into homes, but "good" homes. This suggestion has some appeal. And while it should ultimately be the agency's goal, in the immediate cost-benefit analysis, I think it would be a mistake to do so at this time. While the shelter should ensure potential adopters do not have a history of cruelty, the shelter is not capable of thoughtful adoption screening and the end result will mean the needless loss of animal life.
>
> At this point in the shelter's history, the goal must be to get animals out of the shelter where they are continually under the threat of a death sentence. And given the problems with procedure implementation at the shelter, the process will become arbitrary depending on who is in charge of adoptions. There is simply too much at stake for the staff I observed to hold even more power over life and death.
>
> In addition, several high-volume, high-kill shelters have realized that denying people for criteria other than cruelty, would lead them to get animals (likely unsterilized and unvaccinated) from other sources, with no information or guidance on proper care, which the shelter can still provide.
>
> When the shelter has high quality staff, is consistent in applying sound policies and procedures, and has achieved a higher save rate—when shelter animals do not face certain death—it can revisit the issue of a more thoughtful screening to provide homes more suitable for particular shelter animals.

Unfortunately, too many shelters go too far with fixed, arbitrary rules—dictated by national organizations—that turn away good homes under the theory that people aren't trustworthy, that few people are good enough, and that animals are better off dead. Unfortunately, rescue groups all-too-often share this mindset. But the motivations of rescue groups differ from those of the bureaucrat I ended up firing in Tompkins County. People who do rescue love animals, but they have been schooled by HSUS to be unreasonably—indeed, absurdly—suspicious of the public. Consequently, they make it difficult, if not downright impossible, to adopt their rescued animals.

I recently read the newsletter from a local cat rescue group. There was a story about two cats, Ruby and Alex, in their "happy endings" section. Under the title, "Good things come to those who wait," the story explained that Ruby and Alex were in foster care for 7½ years before they found the "right" home. I wondered what was wrong with the cats. If it took seven years to find them a home, surely they must have had some serious impediments to adoption. But I couldn't find anything in the story. Under another section in the newsletter listing the cats in their care that still needed to find "loving homes," I found the answer.

The first one I looked at was Billy. Billy was a kitten when he was rescued in 2001. He is still in a "foster" home. Does it really take eight years to find the "right" home? Surely, I thought again, something is wrong with this cat. But Billy is described as "easy going, playful, bouncy." It goes on to say that "Billy loves attention and loves to be with his person. Mild-mannered and gentle with new people, he's also a drop-and-roll kitty who will throw himself at your feet to be petted." They also note that he likes dogs. In other words, Billy is perfect.

Clearly, the pertinent question wasn't: "What's wrong with the cats?" The real question was: "What's wrong with these people?" Not surprisingly, the rescue group does not believe families with young children should adopt. They claim that if you have children who are under six years old, you should wait a few years. In reality, this rule is very common in animal sheltering. But it is a mistake nonetheless. Families with children are generally more stable, so they are a highly desirable adoption demographic. They also provide animals with plenty of stimulation, which the animals crave. Children and pets are a match made in heaven.

So if families with children shouldn't adopt, who does that leave? Unfortunately, this group also states that kittens 'require constant supervision like human babies do.' My family frequently fosters kittens for our local shelter. When fostering, we live our lives like we always do: we visit friends, take walks, dine out. We often leave home for hours at a time. Obviously, I would have never done that with my kids when they were babies. That isn't a statement on loving children more than animals. A kitten can sleep, eat, drink, use the litter box, play with a toy, and more at only six weeks of age. A human baby would starve to death surrounded by food if left alone at that age. Kittens are not "like human babies." They are more advanced, skilled, smarter, and cleaner. But that's not the point. The point is that the "constant supervision" rule eliminates potential adopters who go to work, too, but would otherwise provide excellent, loving, nurturing homes. That leaves the two minority extremes: unemployed people and millionaires—although my guess is the former would be ruled out, too.

Having eliminated the two most important adopter demographics (working people and families with children), is it any wonder that Billy—an easy going, playful, cuddly, gentle, drop-and-roll kitty—has been in foster care for eight years?

A Pennsylvania rescue group, operating in a community where animal control kills most animals entering that facility, should be working feverishly to adopt out as many animals as possible so they can open up space to pull more animals from the shelter. Instead, they put up ridiculous roadblocks stating that "Cohabitating couples who have not married need not apply to adopt our pets." Apparently, people have tried because they follow up by noting on their website that you should not waste your time trying because "there are no exceptions." This eliminates many committed couples and, for those who live in states without marriage equality, most gay people.

And a rescue group from Louisiana, a state with some of the highest killing rates in the nation, pummels you with 47 reasons not to adopt an animal on their application, including the warnings that animals will "damage your belongings, soil your furniture and/or flooring, scratch furniture, chew and tear up items, knock down breakable heirlooms, and/or dig up your yard."

When I visited the humane society in Harrisburg, Pennsylvania a number of years ago, I was presented with a list of breeds considered not appropriate for homes with children under ten years old: Chihuahuas, Collies, Toy Breeds, and all small terriers.

Several years ago, this mentality really hit home—literally, my home. We decided to add another dog to our family. Having worked at two of the most successful shelters in the country, having performed rescue my whole adult life, having consulted with some of the largest and best known animal protection groups in the country, owning my own home, working from home, and allowing our dogs the run of the house, I thought adoption would be easy.

Adopting from our local shelter was not possible because we wanted a bigger dog which was against their rules because we had young children. Instead, we searched the online websites, and found a seven year old black Labrador Retriever with a rescue group about an hour south of us. I called about the dog and asked if we could meet him. They wanted to know if we had a "doggy door" leading to the backyard. We did not, but I told them happily—and naively—that I work from home and that we homeschool the kids, so the dog will be with us *all the time*. One of us will just let him out when he wants to go like we do for the resident dogs and then he can come back in. We have a fenced backyard. I housetrained every dog we ever had. No problem, I told them.

But that was not good enough. Apparently, the dog should be able to go in and out whenever he wants without having to ask. No doggy door, no adoption. "But," I started to stammer: seven years old, larger black dog, sleep on the bed, with us all the time, fenced yard.... DENIED.

We then found another dog, a Lab-cross, with a different rescue group. About five years old, "a couch potato" according to the website. Perfect, I thought. I haven't exercised since I was 18! I'll take the dog for a walk around the block twice a day, but mostly will hang out, 24/7!

"We'd like to meet him," I said when I called.

"There's a $25 charge to be considered above and beyond the adoption fee," they replied.

"No problem. If he likes our dogs, we'll pay whatever it costs."

"No," I was told. "You have to pay the non-refundable fee before you can meet any dog and before we review your application."

"What are your rules for adoption?" I said, not wanting to sink $25 if I was going to be denied because of the age of my kids, because I have brown eyes, or because I am balding.

"We can't discuss that until after you pay the $25."

Exasperated, I hung up.

We finally found a dog—a seven year old, lab-mix with a rescue group two hours from us by car. The fee was $250 to adopt, a pricey sum, but we were approved over the telephone because she was familiar with my work.

I could have given up. Lots of people do. When I tell people what I do for a living, that my work takes me all over the country trying to reform antiquated shelter practices, people constantly tell me how they tried to adopt from a shelter or rescue group, but were denied for entirely illogical reasons. One woman told me of her own failed attempt to adopt a dog and save a life. She owned an art gallery and wanted a dog who would come to work with her every day, just like her previous one who had recently died. The new dog would also have the run of both the house and office. She went to several shelters to adopt, but all of them denied her: she had really young kids and she wanted a large dog, and that was against the rules. She ended up at a breeder because she really wanted a dog, she said sheepishly, thinking I would judge her as having failed. "But I tried..." she trailed off. "The shelters failed you," I replied.

Recently, HSUS launched a campaign to help shelters "educate the public" about adoption policies by creating a poster for shelters to hang in their lobbies. The poster features a chair beneath a light in a cement room. The tagline reads: "What's with all the questions?" and it tells you not to take it personally. Rather than ask shelters to reexamine their own assumptions, HSUS produces a poster of what looks like an interrogation room at Abu Ghraib, instructing potential adopters to simply put up with it. In the process, adopters are turned away. Cats like Billy wait years for a home. And animals are needlessly killed: three million adoptable ones, while shelters peddle the fiction that there aren't enough homes.

In fact, there are plenty of homes. The experience of successful No Kill communities proves it; No Kill communities now thrive across the United States. The data also proves it. Approximately three million dogs and cats that need a home are killed every year. Simultaneously, 17 million people are looking to get a new dog or cat and can be persuaded to adopt from a shelter. And, the number of people shelters turn away because of some arbitrary and bureaucratic process proves it. Like this experience shared with me a few years ago:

I tried to adopt from my local shelter… I found this scared, skinny cat hiding in the back of his cage and I filled out an application. I was turned down because I didn't turn in the paperwork on time, which meant a half hour before closing, but I couldn't get there from work in time to do that. I tried to leave work early the next day, but I called and found out they had already killed the poor cat. I will never go back.

Shelter animals already face formidable obstacles to getting out alive: customer service is often poor, a shelter's location may be remote, adoption hours may be limited, policies may limit the number of days they are held, they can get sick in a shelter, and shelter directors often reject common-sense alternatives to killing. One-third to one-half of all dogs and roughly 60 percent of cats are killed because of these obstacles. Since the animals already face enormous problems, including the constant threat of execution, shelters and rescue groups shouldn't add arbitrary roadblocks. When kind hearted people come to help, shelter bureaucrats shouldn't start out with a presumption that they can't be trusted.

In fact, most of the evidence suggests that the public *can* be trusted. While roughly eight million dogs and cats enter shelters every year, that is a small fraction compared to the 165 million thriving in people's homes. Of those entering shelters, only four percent are seized because of cruelty and neglect. Some people surrender their animals because they are irresponsible, but others do so because they have nowhere else to turn—a person dies, they lose their job, their home is foreclosed. In theory, that is why shelters exist—to be a safety net for animals whose caretakers no longer can or want to care for them.

When people decide to adopt from a shelter—despite having more convenient options such as buying from a pet store or responding to a newspaper ad—they should be rewarded. We are a nation of animal lovers, and we should be treated with gratitude, not suspicion. More importantly, the animals facing death deserve the second chance that many well intentioned Americans are eager to give them, but in too many cases, are senselessly prevented from doing so.

The Myth of
Pet Overpopulation

SINCE ITS RELEASE in September 2007, *Redemption: The Myth of Pet Overpopulation & The No Kill Revolution in America* has become the most critically acclaimed book written on its topic. Not only has the book helped shift the national debate about killing; it also plays a direct role in transforming communities. A shelter manager in Washington says the book completely changed her views and she is committing herself to saving all animals in her shelter. Another in Ohio reported that the book gave her the "conviction to move forward" with her No Kill ambitions. Yet another in Louisiana reported to her staff, "We've been doing it wrong, and we are going to start doing it right."

After reading *Redemption*, county commissioners in an Indiana community succeeded in taking to No Kill a shelter that previously killed the vast majority of dogs and cats, often cruelly. As *Redemption* celebrates its continuing success, Tompkins County, New York, finished its seventh No Kill year, Charlottesville, Virginia, entered its third and new communities like those in Reno, Nevada, embraced the No Kill philosophy.

Other communities have also achieved No Kill or are aggressively moving in that direction. No Kill is on the agenda of local governments nation- wide as advocates in communities as diverse as Seattle, Washington, and Indianapolis, Indiana, are using the *Redemption* model to force changes in local shelters.

There have been other notable changes as well. The Humane Society of the United States' favorite misnomer, "euthanasia," has lost its cache. Rescue groups and animal advocates have stopped using it and other HSUS euphemisms such as "putting them to sleep" to describe the abhorrent practice of systematic shelter killing. People are more aware of widespread mistreatment of animals in shelters. And they are less tolerant of the poor care and the killing, the endless excuses to justify it, and the legitimacy that groups like HSUS give to it. The large national humane groups are now on the defensive, softening their anti-No Kill positions and claiming credit for the decline in killing nationally even as they opposed—and in some cases, continue to oppose—the programs responsible for it.

Redemption debunks the myth of pet overpopulation and blames those truly responsible: the very shelter directors who find killing easier than doing what is necessary to stop it, local governments who continue to un- derfund their shelters or place them under the regressive oversight of health and police departments, and shelter managers who protect uncaring and even cruel staff members at the expense of the animals.

Moreover, average people are now aware that shelters kill. And they are aware that there are other shelters and communities that do not kill. After reading the book, one animal lover in Los Angeles, California, told me: "At least now we know what—or more accurately, who—the problem is." We also know how to make them stop. And in more communities na- tionwide, we have.

Unfortunately, many shelter directors refuse to embrace the No Kill paradigm. To them, the culprit for the killing remains "pet overpopula- tion," a dogma they cling to with the fervor of religious faith and which they deem to be simply beyond question—outside the realm of factual confirmation, data, and analysis.

When I argue that pet overpopulation is a myth, I am not saying that some people aren't irresponsible with animals. It doesn't mean that fewer animals entering shelters is not desirable. Nor am I saying shelters don't have institutional obstacles to success. But it *does* mean that these problems are not insurmountable. And it means we can end killing for all savable animals right now—*today*—if all shelter directors cultivate the desire and will to do so, and then earnestly follow through. That is good news—news we should celebrate. And it should be the focal point with which we target our advocacy efforts to achieve the greatest declines in killing possible in the shortest amount of time.

Current estimates from many groups indicate that roughly four million dogs and cats are killed in shelters yearly. Of these, given data on the incidence of aggression in dogs (based on dog bite extrapolation) and save rates at the best performing shelters in the country from diverse regions and demographics, over 90 percent of all shelter animals are "savable." The remaining animals are hopelessly ill or injured animals and vicious dogs whose prognosis for rehabilitation is poor or grave. That would put the number of savable dogs and cats at roughly 3.6 million.

Therefore, we need to increase the market for shelter pets by only three percent in order to *eliminate* killing. Today, there are about 165 million dogs and cats in homes. Of those, less than 20 percent come from shelters. Three percent of 165 million equates to 4.9 million, more than all the savable animals killed in shelters. This is a combination of what statisticians call "stock" and "flow." In layman's terms, some of the market will be replacement life (someone's dog or cat dies or runs away), some of that will be expanding markets (someone doesn't have a dog or cat but wants one, or someone has a dog or cat but wants another one). But it all comes down to increasing where people get their dogs or cats.

These same demographics also tell us that every year, over 20 million people are looking to bring a new dog or cat into their home, more than the total number of dogs and cats entering shelters. Of these, 17 million have not decided where that animal is going to come from and can be persuaded to adopt from a shelter. On top of that, not all animals entering shelters need adoption: Some will be lost strays reclaimed by their family (shelters which are comprehensive in their lost pet reclaim efforts, for example, have demonstrated that as many as two-thirds of stray dogs can be reunited with their families). Others are unsocialized feral cats who should be neutered and released. Some will be vicious dogs or are irremediably suffering. In the end, a shelter needs to find new homes for roughly half of all incoming animals.

Even one of the chief architects of the current paradigm of killing—the Humane Society of the United States—conceded in late 2008 that "increasing the percentage of people who obtain their pets through adoption—by just a few percentage points—we can solve the problem of euthanasia of healthy and treatable dogs and cats."* All the data point to the same conclusion, and even HSUS can no longer deny it.

From the perspective of achievability, therefore, the prognosis for widespread No Kill success is excellent. And we have achieved these results in communities throughout the country. Some are urban, some rural, some in the North, some in the South, some in what we call "liberal" states, and some are in very conservative parts of the country. Demographically, these communities share little in common. However, they do share shelter leadership committed to saving all the lives at risk. And they are proving the validity of the data, which shows that it can be done.

Statistics aside, the fundamental lesson from these communities is that the decisions of shelter managers are the most significant variables in whether animals live or die. Several communities have more than doubled adoptions and cut killing by as much as 75 percent—and it didn't take them five years or more to do it. They did it virtually overnight. In Reno, Nevada, for example, the Nevada Humane Society has increased adoptions as much as 80 percent and reduced killing by over 50 percent, despite taking in a combined 16,000 dogs and cats a year

---

* Unfortunately, while HSUS may have a new language, they still continue to act in old ways. In April of 2008, Randolph, Iowa officials announced a bounty on stray cats, offering residents $5.00 for every cat they rounded up and brought to the shelter to be killed. While cat lovers protested, HSUS officials said they "didn't have a problem with humanely killing a stray cat." In 2007, HSUS asked the King County Council in Washington not to vote on a measure to mandate an 85 percent rate of lifesaving at its animal control shelter, setting itself up against animal activists working to reform that shelter. In August of 2008, HSUS defended the decision by the Hammond, Louisiana animal control shelter to kill every single animal in its facility. And in February of 2009, they supported the mass killing of 145 dogs, including roughly sixty puppies, in a North Carolina shelter despite rescue groups offering to help save them.

with Washoe County Regional Animal Services. Reno's success occurred *immediately* after the hiring of a new shelter director committed
to No Kill and passionate about saving lives. Her appointment followed
the 20-plus year reign of a HSUS darling—a member of their national
sheltering committee—who for two decades found killing animals easier than saving them.

In addition to the speed with which it was attained, what also makes
Reno's success so impressive is that the community takes in over two
times the number of animals per capita than the national average, over
three times the rate of Los Angeles, and five times the San Francisco rate.
If "pet overpopulation" were really a problem, it would be a problem in
Reno. But in 2007, 92 percent of all dogs and 78 percent of all cats were
saved countywide, and in 2008 and again in 2009 Washoe County become one of the safest community for homeless cats in the U.S.—despite
an economic and foreclosure crisis that hit the community hard. With a
lifesaving rate of roughly 90 percent, they are proving that committed
shelters can quickly save the vast majority of animals, even in the face of
public irresponsibility or economic crisis.

WHAT IF PET OVERPOPULATION IS REAL?

But let's put all this aside. Let's assume "pet overpopulation" is real and
insurmountable. To do that, we must ignore the data. We also must ignore
the experiences of successful communities. We must pretend the knowledge and results do not exist.

How does this change our support for the No Kill philosophy? It
doesn't. Shelters nationally are killing roughly half or more of all incoming animals. If I may borrow from an overused sports analogy: we're
at the 50-yard line. And although the evidence is overwhelming to the
contrary, let's say that we can never cross the goal line because of "pet
overpopulation." What is wrong with moving the ball forward? If all shelters put in place the programs and services of the No Kill Equation, we
can save millions of lives nationally, regardless of whether or not we ever
achieve an entirely No Kill nation. Even if people do not believe, as I do,
that a No Kill nation is inevitable, that is worth doing without delay. Every
year we delay, indeed every day we delay, the body count increases. It is

indefensible for shelter directors to refuse to implement programs that would dramatically lower death rates at their shelter simply because they claim those programs cannot eliminate killing entirely.

THE RIGHT TO LIVE

Even if we were simply to surrender reality and conclude that killing savable animals cannot be ended, killing animals would still not be ethical, merciful, or defensible. Animal lovers would still be morally bound to reject it. Any "practical" or utilitarian consideration about killing cannot hold sway over an animal's right to live. Just as other social movements reject the "practical" when it violates the rights of individuals for which they advocate, we, too, should reject the idea that killing animals is acceptable because of the claim that there are "too many" for the "too few" homes which are available." Simply put, killing healthy or treatable animals is immoral.

Indeed, it does not follow that killing of any hopelessly ill, injured or vicious animal is actually ethical. Most animal advocates are not calling for irremediably suffering sheltered animals to be put up for adoption while irremediably suffering because that is cruel. And few, if any, are calling for truly vicious dogs to be adopted into homes in the community because that is dangerous. While over 90 percent of dogs and cats entering shelters would fall outside this limited range of exceptions, it does not follow that the remainder should be killed. While fewer than 10 percent of shelter animals may not be healthy or treatable, the vast majority of those are not suffering. This might include a dog with cancer whose prognosis is grave, but who still has a good quality of life for a limited time. It might include a cat with renal disease in its early stages. In fact, these animals live without pain, at least until they succumb to their illness.

Today, the great challenge in sheltering is between No Kill advocates working to ensure that healthy animals, animals with treatable medical conditions, and feral animals, are no longer killed in shelters and the defenders of tradition who claim that killing animals under the guise of "euthanasia" is necessary and proper. As the No Kill paradigm becomes more established, however, the humane movement will have to confront other ethical quandaries within our philosophy.

These ethical quandaries include: killing dogs who are aggressive but can lead happy lives in sanctuaries where they cannot harm the public; and killing hopelessly ill animals rather than giving them hospice care. Even today, the idea of killing *at all* is challenged by a small but growing movement of sanctuaries and hospice care groups. They argue for a "third door" between adoption and killing. That these issues have not yet been rigorously debated within the No Kill movement does not mean they shouldn't be. They should. Compassion must be embraced whenever it presents itself, especially when it furthers an animal's right to live.

DISMANTLING THE KILLING PARADIGM

Realistically, however, if I can come back to my sports analogy: we will cross the goal line and achieve a No Kill nation. To paraphrase abolitionist Theodore Parker and Martin Luther King, Jr., the arc of history may be wide, but it bends toward greater justice and compassion. And compassion dictates we will get there. But to do that, we must dismantle the current paradigm that says it is acceptable to adopt out only a precious few and systematically kill the rest, a paradigm long championed by the very institutions that should have been working to create a No Kill nation. Beginning over 40 years ago with their first Vice President of Companion Animals, Phyllis Wright, the Humane Society of the United States abandoned what should have been its primary mission: ending the killing of animals in shelters. Instead, HSUS championed a philosophy that excused killing, often promoted it, and cemented its hegemony; at the expense of the animals.

In her seminal and cataclysmic essay "Why We Must Euthanize," Wright wrote that she "put 70,000 dogs and cats to sleep.... But I tell you one thing: I don't worry about one of those animals that were put to sleep." The essay not only coined one of the biggest misnomers of them all ("putting them to sleep") and created an emotionally acceptable pretext for killing; it helped cement the paradigm that allows groups like HSUS to claim that killing is morally acceptable, indeed an imperative. Wright's world-view informs HSUS' historical and present positions, including the myths that no one wants to kill, that killing is the public's fault, that killing is kindness, and that shelters have no choice in the matter—all positions proven false. These have been the backbone of the paradigm responsible for the mass extermination of dogs and cats. Every animal who enters a U.S. shelter today faces the very real potential for being killed as a direct result of the broken animal shelter system HSUS helped to create.

That paradigm not only shuts the door to No Kill in many communities, but it also undermines all the other goals that groups like HSUS should support. To defend the killing of healthy and treatable animals and refer to it as "euthanasia," or "putting them to sleep," or "moral," or "ethical," or "necessary," or "kind," or "proper," obscures the truth and the ends they should be seeking.

The right to life is universally acknowledged as basic or fundamental. It is basic or fundamental because the enjoyment of the right to life is a necessary condition of the enjoyment of all other rights. No "right" is guaranteed when it can be taken away by killing. A movement cannot be "rights" oriented, as many of these groups claim to be, yet ignore the right to life. By asserting that humans have the right to deny animals their lives, they make the attainment of any animal rights inherently impossible.

In both a philosophical and absolute sense, animals have only their lives. If life is taken, nothing is left. Once they are killed, these animals can no longer think and feel and run and play and eat and sleep and purr and bark and love and be loved. It is over. Forever.

In failing to champion the right of dogs and cats to live, these organizations also miss the opportunity to harness the public's progressive attitudes and great love for animals. It is that love and compassion that could yield laws banning killing in animal shelters altogether. This achievement—securing a legally guaranteed right to life for a species of non-human animal—will be a seminal event, a crossing of the Rubicon from which our society will never return. As history and the human rights movement predict, that door—once opened—will be forced open even wider to accommodate other species of animals currently exploited or killed in other contexts.

Right now, however, the nation's largest self-proclaimed "animal rights" groups, including HSUS and People for the Ethical Treatment of Animals, are fighting to keep that door closed—by arguing that dogs and

THE MYTH OF PET OVERPOPULATION

cats do not have the right to life and by telling us, in some variation or another, that "killing is kindness," "killing is not killing," and even that "killing is a gift." It is beyond irony. It is beyond hypocrisy. It is beyond betrayal. It is beyond self-defeating. It is insane.

Groups like PETA may claim to be leaders of the animal rights move-ment, and the larger public may equate animal rights with PETA, but their positions and actions demonstrate otherwise. By claiming to be "animal rights" advocates while advocating for the right of humans to kill animals and killing animals themselves in staggering numbers,* they advance hypocritical, irreconcilable propositions that result in a deadly double standard that is—at its very core—antithetical to their proclaimed mis-sion. Because the treatment they condone, encourage, and even practice for animals is treatment they would never accept for themselves, given that no one—and I mean not one solitary person on the planet—would be an advocate for killing if they themselves unnecessarily faced the needle.

RECLAIMING OUR MOVEMENT

Thankfully, the public is increasingly aware of just how broken our shel-ter system is and supports the No Kill alternative. Not only do approxi-mately 165 million dogs and cats share our homes, and not only are we spending nearly $50 billion per year on their care and comfort, but study after study confirms that people sacrifice during an economic downturn, rather than curtail care for their animal companions. Indeed, the average American is far more progressive about dogs and cats than every animal welfare and animal rights organization in the United States, with rare ex-ception. The success of No Kill does not depend on winning the hearts and

---

* In 2006, PETA took in 3,043 animals and killed 2,981 of them. Despite nearly $30 mil-lion in revenues, and millions of animal loving supporters, they killed 97 percent of the animals. In 2007, despite record rates of lifesaving in shelters which take in thousands more animals at a fraction of PETA's budget and despite that new figures report that rates of shelter killing dropped to their lowest levels ever as more shelters embraced the lifesav-ing programs of the No Kill Equation, PETA's killing showed little sign of subsiding. PETA killed roughly 91 percent of the animals they impounded, taking in 1,997 and putting 1,815 to death.

minds of the American public. We don't need to gain their support; we have
it already. While the voices of tradition chant "kill, kill, kill," most dog and
cat lovers, armed with the facts, find it abhorrent.

We must therefore recognize that the battle to save companion animals is not against the public: the battle is within. Our battle is against the
cowards of our movement who refuse to stand up to their colleagues and
friends running shelters that are mired in the failed and defunct philosophies that allow (indeed, cause) killing. Our battle is against those who
claim to be part of our movement but fail to recognize the yearly killing
of millions of animals as an unnecessary and cruel slaughter and to call it
what it is. It is against those who will not do for the animals that which is
their solemn duty to do: to change themselves and to demand that their
colleagues change, when that is what the situation demands.

The only thing standing between today's system of mass killing and
the No Kill nation we can immediately achieve is the leaders of the large
national organizations who refuse to seize the opportunity. Instead, they
are determined to fail—to ensure that the paradigm they have championed
for so long is not upended—by blocking reform efforts that challenge their
hegemony; by protecting and defending both draconian shelter practices
and uncaring shelter directors; and by squandering the potential repre-
sented by the great love people have for companion animals.

By contrast, what would the large national groups be doing different-
ly if they embraced No Kill? In practice, it means reporting to the public
and shelter administrators that No Kill has been achieved, requiring full
implementation of the No Kill Equation, and demanding the removal of
shelter managers who refuse to do so. It means promoting the communities that have achieved levels of No Kill success that others have not. It
means arguing in all publications, advocacy efforts, educational materi-
als, media interactions and conferences that No Kill is the only legitimate
standard for animal sheltering—and must be *immediately* embraced by
all shelters. It means stating unequivocally that shelters must modernize
and innovate by replacing century old practices with the life-affirming
programs and services of the No Kill Equation. It means assisting activists trying to reform their shelters rather than fighting them—even when
doing so means confronting a fractious shelter director who refuses to

change. It means no longer rewarding failing shelter directors with speaking engagements at their conferences, with features in their magazines, with national awards, or with hundreds of thousands of dollars to be squandered. That, of course, would be quickly followed by investing their huge resources in lobbying for and funding change in communities, including a widespread effort to reform shelters, remove entrenched kill-oriented directors, and provide necessary infrastructure.

With a group like HSUS leading the charge, our nation could very easily outlaw the shelter killing of savable companion animals. If one of these organizations were to champion such a law in any given community, who would dare oppose? What animal control director could stand up against HSUS political muscle and the will of their community? Who would be left to legitimize their refusal to change or to parrot their diversionary platitudes about public irresponsibility, pet overpopulation, or the need to kill?

Only time will tell how long allegiance to their kill-oriented colleagues, to their antiquated philosophies, and to their failed models, will hold them back from the success they and this movement can achieve the moment they decide to embrace it.

Rethinking Animal
Control Contracts

HUMANE SOCIETIES and SPCAs are synonymous in people's minds with animal control shelters, so the public often has difficulty separating the two functions. But animal control—protecting people from the *perceived* public health and safety threats caused by animals—is not why SPCAs were founded. Although each SPCA and humane society is a unique entity with its own funding, policies, and governance structure, most of them have similar histories. Many were founded in the late 19th and early 20th centuries, primarily to prosecute cruelty and provide water troughs for overworked horses. Many also turned their attention to the cruelties inflicted by local dogcatchers, including the theft of dogs to sell at the pound, withholding food to realize greater profits, and cruel methods of killing.

The 19th century ASPCA in New York City, led by its founder, Henry Bergh, was one of the most zealous of these organizations. Intense ASPCA opposition helped defeat New York City's proposed law requiring all dogs to be muzzled in public. And thanks to Bergh, specific breeds outlawed in many states and ordered killed on sight in others were not banned in New York City during this time. Under Bergh's leadership, the ASPCA prosecuted cruelty cases against city dogcatchers. And Bergh's tenacity even led to the christening of a more modern dog pound facility.

Tired of fighting with the ASPCA, New York City's aldermen asked the Society to run the dog pound. Henry Bergh refused. He believed the ASPCA should protect life, not end it. He believed that the ASPCA's role to protect *animals* from *people* was fundamentally at odds with that of a pound. Bergh understood that animal welfare and animal control served two distinct purposes, in conflict on issues of life and death. This tension can be reduced but never eliminated. Bergh's answer was clear. "This Society," he wrote, "could not stultify its principles so far as to encourage the tortures which the proposed give rise to." Henry Bergh would not allow his ASPCA to do the city's bidding in killing dogs they deemed "unwanted."

THE ROAD MOST TRAVELED

Following Bergh's death—and contrary to his wishes—the ASPCA capitulated and accepted a contract to operate New York City's dog pound. It was a tragic mistake. In little more than a decade, running the pound became the ASPCA's primary role. By 1910, the ASPCA did little more than impound dogs and cats on behalf of the city, with nearly all put to death. Within a short period of time, the many SPCAs that were formed around the country and modeled themselves after the ASPCA—though independent and distinct—nonetheless followed suit. The guaranteed income provided by contracts helped sway many SPCAs and humane societies to abandon their traditional platforms of animal advocacy and cruelty prosecutions in favor of administering dog control for cities and counties. Within a decade or two, most mainstream humane societies did little more than kill dogs and cats.

After a century of humane societies performing pound work for their municipalities, we live in a nation where the organizations founded to save animals kill them. We live in a nation where the very institutions that should attack the lethal paradigm instead defend it. We live in a nation where the very institutions that should legally challenge anti-animal laws enforce them. And we live in a nation where the SPCAs and humane societies, which should be unequivocal advocates for lifesaving, fight those who are.

Until recently, this paradigm of sheltering remained unchallenged.

With the rise of the No Kill movement in the 1990s, animal lovers started demanding that shelters stop killing. In response, many of these shelters counter that they have no choice but to continue doing so. Calling themselves "open door animal control shelters," these organizations argue that the contractual obligation to take in all animals means they *must* kill. This was proven false when the Tompkins County SPCA, which served as the animal control authority for the entire county and was legally mandated to accept all animals, spearheaded the first No Kill community in the United States. Other shelters—both municipal and those working under animal control contracts—have since reaffirmed that "open door" shelters can be No Kill.

Now that the Tompkins County SPCA is considering relinquishing the contract based on the costs of doing so, those who remain hostile to No Kill argue that No Kill is financially unsustainable. This is simply not true. The legal mandate to provide animal control services rests with government; the Tompkins County SPCA has performed the service under contract as many private humane societies do. For far too many years, however, local government underpaid for the service. Critics of No Kill ignore that the Tompkins County SPCA was No Kill for seven years while receiving animal control funding that was less than one-fourth of what groups like the Humane Society of the United States recommend for municipalities and far less than the national average. If anything, these facts validate the viability of No Kill. Unfortunately, while costs have increased over the last several years (as they have in every other sector of our economy), animal control funding has not. When the Tompkins County SPCA asked for a modest fee increase to make the arrangement more equitable, some town administrators refused.

If this was any other shelter, groups like HSUS would have rallied around it: its request for an increase from $1.65 to $3.00 per capita would remain well below the $5.00 to $7.00 HSUS recommends for shelters nationally, and far less than surrounding counties pay for traditional, kill-oriented animal control. But because Tompkins County SPCA symbolizes No Kill, critics use the situation to attack No Kill as financially unsustainable—a deceitful double standard. Every private shelter performing animal control in every community needs to periodically renegotiate the terms of their contract to keep pace with higher costs. This is no different than municipal shelters asking for increases in their budgets as costs also increase.

But the move away from animal control transcends the issue of No Kill. Kill shelters, too, are relinquishing their animal control contracts due to inadequate compensation. They are surrendering the contract back to the municipalities they have served for the same reason that the San Francisco SPCA did so in 1989. According to then-President Richard Avanzino, "the [SPCA] was in a battle with the City over funding. And it appeared that this battle would never end (and it didn't). The City wasn't providing us with enough money to adequately do the job. Increasingly, we had to make up the difference with charitable dollars."

Private SPCAs and humane societies have subsidized animal control for so long that it has become the unfair expectation of municipalities that these private non-profits should continue to do so. Assuming that the agencies will retain these contracts regardless of whether or not they cover the actual costs of running animal control, and regardless of whether they are No Kill or killing shelters, governments force shelters to use private donations to subsidize a government mandate. Consequently, these shelters are using money raised for adoptions and other lifesaving work to pay the cost of enforcing often arcane and inhumane animal laws (e.g., breed bans, leash laws, feeding bans, pet limit laws). No Kill or not, many shelters nationwide are becoming increasingly intolerant of this burden.

In Tompkins County, the SPCA simply wanted government to cover actual costs of providing enforcement and care of the animals during the minimum holding period. This came out to about $3.00 per capita, less than what surrounding municipalities in other counties pay (approximately $5.00 per capita) for kill shelters. Likewise, the Charlottesville SPCA has subsidized animal control costs for decades, even during a period in its history when it was hostile to the No Kill philosophy and widely criticized by the rescue community for unnecessary killing. It is currently renegotiating its $1.50 per capita contract for animal control because it does not cover the actual cost of providing the service. And they are not alone. Around the country, shelters have relinquished their contracts for animal control for the same reason, with the vast majority of these being neither No Kill nor supportive of the philosophy. These include, for example, shelters in New York, Pennsylvania, California, Maryland, Washington, and Mississippi.

It would be tragic if bureaucrats continue to dig in their heels and force progressive shelters running No Kill animal control programs to abandon their contracts at this time; it is probable that whatever agency assumes the responsibility will not have a No Kill orientation. However, no agency can indefinitely spend more in animal control than it is paid for the service—and this is true if the agency is progressive or reactionary, killing or not killing.

Even HSUS has supported the idea of kill-oriented shelters leaving animal control work when "humane organizations end up in tenuous financial positions that threaten their standards of operation" because of insufficient government funding. HSUS suggests that shelters should never "get to the point where [their] private programs or [their] real mission is undermined by the public health needs [which are the responsible of local government, not private humane societies]."

Ironically, once they stop contracting with a private humane society for these services, many municipalities assume the function themselves and discover that their costs are two or more times higher than the modest contract amount requested by humane societies. In 1990, the San Francisco Board of Supervisors learned too late what a bargain the San Francisco SPCA had been, and ended up paying millions more annually for the city to run the program. When the Pennsylvania SPCA first walked away from animal control several years ago, the city was paying $790,000 per year for the service, about 54 cents per capita and the lowest of the largest cities in the United States. In its first year as a municipal shelter, the city's budget was over three times as much, and outside evaluations showed that they needed to increase that by several million to run a minimally acceptable program. And not only are these cities paying more; many of these communities often get less service due to bureaucratic intransigence and hostility to the lifesaving endeavor often inherent to local government.

RECLAIMING OUR ROOTS

But there are larger philosophical issues than fair compensation at stake in the debate regarding humane societies and SPCAs administering animal control. Ultimately, it should not be the mission of a private humane society to enforce laws which are antithetical to humane principles. Nor should SPCAs kill animals (even if they limit it to aggressive dogs

and non-savable animals) in the name of a public health mandate issued by government. As I wrote in *Redemption*, insufficient funding was
only part of the equation in San Francisco:

> [Richard Avanzino, then President of the San Francisco SPCA]
> could no longer ignore the fact that his efforts to save animals con-
> tradicted the city's mandate to run the pound. Avanzino's SPCA was
> wearing two hats—the lifesaving hat of the SPCA, and the other of the
> city pound. On the one hand, he worked to save animals by spaying and
> neutering them, fostering them, and taking them offsite for adoption;
> on the other hand, his organization killed them on behalf of the city. He
> grew weary of the contradiction. In 1988, Avanzino signed the society's
> final animal control contract with the city and gave notice that he would
> not renew it the following year. The San Francisco SPCA was ready to
> sever the cord of running animal control.

Until then, virtually every major city had an SPCA or humane
society that contracted for animal control services, and these shelters had become dependent on the revenue streams provided by
animal control contracts, although in most cases they did not provide the level of funding needed to perform the services mandated. As a result, these agencies' private fundraising efforts, which
brought in revenue above and beyond contractual payments from
cities and towns for animal control services, were not being used
to maximize lifesaving. Instead, they were being spent performing
animal control enforcement. Animal lovers who donated to their
local shelter were inadvertently paying officers to write citations,
rather than fund expanding adoption services.

Avanzino was on the verge of walking away from $1.8 million
dollars per year. Of more significance, he was threatening to take
the San Francisco SPCA into uncharted waters. Killing unwanted
pets, intentional or not, had become central to the organizational
imperative of virtually every humane society and SPCA in the country. With "farm animal" slaughter laws now the subject of state and
federal oversight, and draft horses replaced by cars and trains, the
platforms of the late 19th century were now obsolete. After more
than a century of service, animal control thoroughly defined the
soul of the nation's animal shelters.

But Avanzino no longer wanted his SPCA to be a part of it. He
was going to take the San Francisco SPCA back to its roots, to the

founding vision of Henry Bergh's ideal that an SPCA should be a tool for lifesaving, not killing. If a city chose to round up and kill dogs and cats, it was not the SPCA's job to do it for them. Instead, like the ASPCA of Bergh's day, Avanzino's SPCA would provide oversight to make sure that killing was done as humanely as possible, while using its resources and advocacy efforts to reduce it as much as possible.

Consequently, the "animal control" functions Avanzino saw as antithetical to the mission of an organization dedicated to advocacy on behalf of animals—impoundment of vicious animals and city ordinance enforcement (including ticketing for dog license violations, leash laws, and "pooper scooper" laws)—would go back to the City.

Although an SPCA seeking to turn its community No Kill can do so under contract for animal control, it need not be in that position to effect change. After the San Francisco SPCA relinquished its animal control contract, it took up the charge to achieve a No Kill city. Using a groundswell of public support, Avanzino's SPCA succeeded in forcing the city animal control director to participate in a plan that ended the killing of healthy animals. And just as there are many progressive SPCAs and regressive animal control shelters in communities nationwide, there are also progressive animal control shelters and regressive SPCAs. In 2005, for example, it was the Philadelphia Animal Care & Control Association that supported Trap-Neuter-Release programs for feral cats; while the then-director of the Pennsylvania SPCA opposed them. As always, it is the leadership—not the labels of the organizations—that determines their commitment to and success at lifesaving.

WHERE DO WE GO FROM HERE?

I am not suggesting that all SPCAs should abandon animal control today. In King County, Washington, for example, animal advocates are pushing for a private organization to take over the animal control function after several independent assessments showed King County Animal Care & Control subjects animals to neglect, cruelty, and kills in the face of alternatives. In Tompkins County during my tenure, we ran animal control and saved 93 percent of all animals. In Charlottesville, Virginia, the SPCA also saves 90 percent of all animals while running animal control. In an imperfect world, communities must choose the scenario likely to save the most animals in its particular circumstances.

As a result, the calculus isn't cut and dried. And the answer to the question of whether or not a private humane society should administer animal control in any given community is not absolute *at this time in history*. Our ultimate goal should be the ideal—private SPCAs doing truly humane work, local government humanely administering public health and safety programs, and the two working in concert to save all the lives at risk. San Francisco held out the right promise in the 1990s, even though local leaders prevented its achievement and have since abandoned the goal.

But today, in some communities across the United States, the local SPCA can and should run animal control because it can do so and retain its No Kill orientation, and because the alternative is a return to unnecessary killing. In other communities, municipal animal control directors lead the charge toward No Kill. Because of historical hostility to No Kill by many SPCAs and humane societies, contracting out services might lead to more killing.

So we must always be pragmatic in our strategy, assessing the political landscape of each community independently to determine the appropriate course of action. But we must also always keep in mind the No Kill movement's ultimate goal—building the foundation needed to redirect our nation's private SPCAs and humane societies away from animal control and back to the philosophy that motivated the movement's founders.

The sooner we end the era when private shelters kill animals on behalf of government, the sooner we will reclaim our movement. And the sooner we do that, the closer we will be not only to creating a No Kill nation, but also to sustaining it in perpetuity.

What is True Euthanasia?

Two MEMBERS of our family died this year of cancer. We lost our cat, Gina, to squamous cell carcinoma. And my wife lost an uncle, Steve,* to lung cancer. Both were surrounded by people committed to minimizing any pain or discomfort during the last weeks of their life. Both were surrounded by the people they loved and who loved them when they died. But their deaths could not have been more different. We "euthanized" Gina. Steve was allowed to die naturally. And this difference has raised significant ethical issues, which I am trying to sort out.

In the past, I've never had an ethical dilemma with euthanasia for end of life in my irremediably suffering animal companions. I never hastily made the decision and have always waited until the very end, using "euthanasia" to prevent my companion animals from experiencing what I hope are only the last hours or, at most, day or two of suffering before they would die naturally. I do not believe it is acceptable to kill an animal at the point of a grave diagnosis or when death is not imminent;

---

* Steve's name has been changed to protect the privacy of his immediate family.

the open question is at the end-stages of a terminal disease when the
animal deeply suffers. Only under those circumstances have I ever believed in the morality of such a decision. In other words, it is only when
I have been certain that death was truly imminent that I have chosen to
"euthanize"—to spare my animals the last, painful moments of their bodies shutting down.

And in my advocacy for a No Kill nation, I have often said that our
goal in sheltering is to bring "euthanasia" back to its dictionary definition: "the act or practice of killing or permitting the death of hopelessly
sick or injured individuals in a relatively painless way for reasons of mercy." I've tended to focus on the first part: "the act of killing" as opposed
to the second, "permitting the death." But the vivid contrast between the
deaths of two members of my family, from the same disease simultaneously, has sharpened this issue for me.

That doesn't mean that I am second guessing the goals of the No Kill
movement *at this time in history*. Today, the No Kill movement seeks to
save all healthy and treatable animals, including ferals. Together, they
comprise roughly 95 percent of shelter intakes in the United States. But
the fact that the others are hopelessly ill, irremediably suffering, or vicious dogs doesn't mean their killing isn't ethically problematic.

Truth be told, some of those in the remaining small percent are not
suffering, so their killing raises a host of ethical issues. Some of these
animals are living without pain, and can continue to do so, at least for a
time. And in regards to aggressive dogs, the fact that shelters cannot and
should not adopt them out does not mean that their killing isn't ethically
problematic.

Right now, our great challenge in sheltering is between No Kill advocates who seek to modernize shelters and the archaic voices of tradition
that say "killing is kindness." Once those latter voices are silenced and
No Kill's hegemony is established, we will have to confront ethical quandaries within our own philosophy. These ethical quandaries include:
killing dogs who are aggressive but can lead happy lives in sanctuaries
where they cannot harm the public; and killing hopelessly ill animals
rather than giving them hospice care. At the end of the day, we deceive

ourselves when we think our ethical analysis will not change as our society offers greater compassion and rights for animals.

I believe one of the debates we must have on a larger scale is the issue of "euthanasia," even when it meets the dictionary definition. The question being: *Is the idea of mercy killing always ethical?* That it is not may be difficult to grasp when healthy animals are killed under the notion of "euthanasia" with the full support of groups like the American Veterinary Medical Association, the Humane Society of the United States, and even self-proclaimed animal lovers and animal activists. But the question should be proposed and evaluated thoughtfully, without a knee-jerk dismissal, or the regurgitation of platitudes that obscure more than they illuminate and provide apologia before real reflection begins.

When Gina was nearing the end of her life, I faced a new dilemma that we haven't really fully debated as a society or as a movement, although compassionate people are asking those questions more often—and some people have been asking them for a very long time. When human medicine determined that nothing more could be done for Steve, they turned to hospice care: to keeping Steve pain-free, as comfortable as possible, and in his home, surrounded by people he loved and who loved him. His hospice care nurse was well-trained and compassionate, and when she knew death was near, she asked that family come to say good-bye. Steve died peacefully, and without pain, surrounded by the people he loved.

As they did when Steve learned he had cancer, we were very aggressive with treatment when Gina was diagnosed, including chemotherapy, steroids, antibiotics for the secondary infections, and fluid therapy. And as they did with Steve, when the disease progressed and Gina stopped eating altogether, we sought comfort measures only, including pain killers. In fact, in doing research about how people make the decision to take humans off of life-support to see if there was an analog for Gina, I found the decision making process in that context lacked rigor. We are clumsy in terms of making the decision for people; I shouldn't have been surprised to find we are even clumsier in making these decisions for our animal companions. Platitudes about "quality of life *versus* quantity of life" lack integrity when they replace critical and scientific analysis. And

that—along with preemptive absolution that end-of-life euthanasia was
a "gift"—is all I seemed to find. I was unprepared to make the call to end
her life, as I had with other companion animals. Part of the dilemma
was that Gina was the most resolute cat I've ever known. She was ada-
mant. No, she would not use a litter box. No, she would not stay upstairs.
No, she would not stay downstairs. No, she would not stay indoors. No,
she would not stay outdoors. No, she would not stop using the couch to
sharpen her claws. Gina was the ultimate in personality and mischief: an
individual with a set beliefs and practices that made her uniquely Gina.
And that made her full of life. How can you take that away? But the best
laid plans...

On a day when she looked really bad, when she had not eaten in a
week, when she stumbled while walking, when she urinated and defecat-
ed on herself, when she no longer wanted to get up, when she no longer
took comfort in being petted or held, and with a fear raging that we were
prolonged her suffering by keeping her alive with fluids, long after she
would have died on her own of dehydration (though no such concerns
were presented about Steve despite the fact that he stopped eating weeks
earlier), our determination to let her die naturally slipped away. There
would be no "permitting the death of hopelessly sick or injured individuals in a relatively painless way for reasons of mercy." We would follow the
traditional "act or practice of killing," although for the same reason.

The veterinarian was compassionate in our taking of what remained
of Gina's life, as she had been during her entire illness. And as we held
her, and told her how much we loved her, and thanked her for sharing her
life with us, we watched as her veterinarian administered the fatal dose.
And she drifted away from us. And I felt like I not only left my beautiful
cat in that room, but a little part of my humanity.

It has been said that rare is the individual who can see beyond the
mores of his or her own time. I've always admired such people and try
to emulate them. Even if I never get there, I strive to. I struggle to. That
is why I read history; to remind myself that those in our past who have
moved us forward were those who continually questioned the accepted values and beliefs of their time, and never let custom or the pervasiveness of a practice deter them from championing what they deduced

to be right. In doing so, they laid out a vision for a more compassionate and ethical future for all of us. And so I continually question, and will continue to question, regardless of what may seem like a practical imperative, whether we go far enough in our actions for and in defense of our companion animal friends and family. It is a tremendous responsibility to speak for the interests of someone else—especially when that someone else cannot speak for themselves, especially when it involves life and death, and especially when it is someone you love, relying on you to champion their best interests.

I continue to struggle about the decision to end Gina's life, and hope I did the right thing. I have been assured by others that I did, but, for the first time in my life, I am not so sure. And I also can't help but think of larger implications; that if hospice care were the norm and people no longer killed their companion animals even at the end-stages of their lives, or at the very least, if doing so was not the common choice, the ramifications for the sanctity of animal life would be tremendous. If the discussion were to unfold as a movement, as a society, within the veterinary community, and carried the same weight and gravity that it evokes when the topic relates to the same issue, but concerns our human family members, the impact on society's tolerance for the mass killing in what we euphemistically call "shelters" (but are often little more than death camps) would be sea-changing. I believe that is what we owe the Ginas who allow us to share our lives with them.

If only she could have answered me that day when I whispered in her ear as we said goodbye to her for the last time, "Sweetheart, is this what you would have wanted?"

We're the Ones We've Been Waiting For

*The Landslide Victory of California's Proposition 2 and the Animal Movement's Own "Bradley Effect"**

BEFORE 2008's historic election and even with then-candidate Barack Obama leading in the polls, Democrats were privately (and not so privately) worrying about what "white America" would do in the privacy of the polling booth. What they did is no longer a mystery.

The New York Times columnist Frank Rich noted that "almost every assumption about America that was taken as a given by our political culture on [election] morning was proved wrong by [election] night." According to Rich:

> The most conspicuous clichés to fall, of course, were the twin suppositions that a decisive number of white Americans wouldn't vote for a black presidential candidate—and that they were lying to

---

* Wikipedia defines the Bradley Effect as "a theory proposed to explain observed discrepancies between voter opinion polls and election outcomes in some U.S. government elections where a white candidate and a non-white candidate run against each other... [T]he theory proposes that some voters tend to tell pollsters that they are undecided or likely to vote for a black candidate, and yet, on election day, vote for his white opponent. It was named after Los Angeles Mayor Tom Bradley, an African-American who lost the 1982 California governor's race despite being ahead in voter polls going into the elections." (Citations omitted.)

pollsters about their rampant racism. But the polls were accurate. There was no "Bradley effect."

In California, there was another equally revealing vote on November 4, 2008. It, too, shattered the myths we hold about the public. The animal movement has been living with its own "Bradley effect," the notion that despite all the evidence to the contrary—the people we see at the dog park, the people we talk to in the lobby of our veterinarian's office, the best-selling books and top box office movies about animals, how much money we spend on our pets, how many of us share our homes with animal companions, the demographics that show the immense compassion of a pet-loving nation—Americans are irresponsible and don't care enough about animals. And, that the corollary to this uncaring is that our shelters have no choice but to kill roughly four million dogs and cats every year.

Thanks to the response by Californians to Proposition 2, that notion has also been proven wrong. Proposition 2 makes it illegal for animals (mostly chickens) on farms to be confined *"in a manner that prevents such animal from: (a) Lying down, standing up, and fully extending his or her limbs; and (b) Turning around freely."* It's a simple law but its reach is extensive, affecting about 90 percent of chicken farms in the country's largest agricultural state. But it is so much more than that.

Proposition 2 is a bellwether of just how enormous the political capital of animals has become. The vote to outlaw battery cages for chickens, where numerous hens are crammed together into spaces the size of a desk drawer, had as its focus protecting animals from the worst abuses of the factory farming system, but its resounding success at the polls has a far greater significance for *all* animals.

Supporters of Proposition 2, including the Humane Society of the United States, which spearheaded the initiative, are quick to point out that this new law (which also impacts how pigs and calves are housed) affects more animals than any ballot measure in U.S. history. But even this reading misses its political significance. The victory of Proposition 2—specifically its *margin of victory*—not only shatters every notion we hold about people's view of animals, but also illustrates the ease with which we could end the pound killing of dogs, cats, and all the other companion animals currently being slaughtered by the millions.

CONVENTIONAL WISDOM
PREDICTED FAILURE

California is our nation's largest agricultural state, and the opposition to Proposition 2, which outspent proponents by a three-to-one margin, argued that its passage would make California economically uncompetitive, would drive people out of business (or out of the state), and would increase the cost of eggs and other "groceries." They also argued it would make "food" less safe.

In addition to industry groups, which spent nine million dollars in opposition, most newspapers around the state also opposed it. *The San Francisco Chronicle*, arguably one of the state's most liberal newspapers, urged its readers to vote against it, parroting industry arguments about its economic impact.

On top of that, political heavyweights in California and beyond came out in opposition, including the California Farm Bureau, the California Small Business Association, and the Mexican American Political Association. Even the U.S. Department of Agriculture weighed in, spending taxpayer money on a campaign to defeat it (until a court ordered it to stop, finding its actions an illegal use of its regulatory power).

And in an argument reeking with racial overtones, some opponents went so far as to pander to the worst elements of our society, claiming it would mean an influx of cheap, unhealthy, and possibly tainted eggs from Mexico—painting the picture of an onslaught of "undesirable" egg immigration from South of the border.

With pre- and exit-polling showing that the economy was the forefront concern on people's minds as they cast their vote over a wide range of issues, including the selection of our next President, conventional wisdom made Proposition 2's prospects appear grim. With roughly three-fourths of voters putting the economy, particularly loss of jobs, as the core issue this election; and, with the mainstream press and the initiative's opponents arguing that Proposition 2 would mean loss of business, loss of jobs, and higher prices, conventional wisdom would dictate that the intent of the law—to give chickens more room in a factory farm—would not trump other concerns in voters' calculations.

But Proposition 2 passed. And it didn't *barely* pass. It passed by the widest margin of any proposition in California, right up there with providing housing assistance to veterans. Roughly 80 percent of all counties in California approved the measure, three-fourths of all voters. By all accounts, it was nothing short of a landslide.

WHY THIS RESULT IS SO IMPORTANT

Success for humane legislation is not limited to California. During the same election, Massachusetts voters ended greyhound racing. In 2007, Oregon voters followed Florida's lead and banned gestation crates for pigs. And in 2006, Arizona voters passed a farm animal protection statute banning veal crates, while Michigan voters defeated a measure to increase hunting. In short, we have discovered that despite all that separates us as Americans, people of all walks of life want to build a better world for animals.

Especially significant is that Proposition 2's victory shows Americans don't just care about dogs and cats; they also care about animals with which they have no personal relationships. And if they care so much despite all the forces urging the defeat of Proposition 2, we need to put to bed, once and for all, the idea that dogs and cats need to die in U.S. shelters because people don't care enough about them.

What it means is that we could end shelter killing altogether if HSUS and other organizations put real effort into doing so—rather than legitimizing and fighting people who are trying to stop it. And we could do so *today*! Such a result would do infinitely more than give animals some elbow room before they are slaughtered, like the chickens covered by Proposition 2. We can actually *save the lives* of millions of animals every year. The prize is there for the taking. It is low-hanging fruit.

And only our movement's own inaction prevents us from doing so: our movement's own failure to stand up to those who would keep it shrouded in darkness, who would squander our donations and reform efforts on trying to make the public bend to our will, when we should be bending to theirs. To borrow a cliché: "We have met the enemy and he is us."

POLITICAL "MUSCLE"

Since new leadership took over the Humane Society of the United States in 2004, its budget has increased from $75 million to nearly $130 million per year, making it the nation's largest and arguably most powerful animal welfare organization. HSUS has amassed enormous resources, media capability, and—to use their own phrase—"political muscle," all of it a reflection of the love people have for animals.

And the lesson of Proposition 2 is that all of this love in all of its manifestations (including HSUS' financial and political largesse) can and should be leveraged to effect change. Specifically, it can be used to end the policy of killing companion animals in shelters. Despite this game-changing size, however, HSUS has proved to be no friend of shelter animals. HSUS leadership continues to provide political cover for shelter killing and fails to acknowledge and promote existing No Kill success while offering only token initiatives toward it.

For example, when public outcry erupted over a decision by a Louisiana HSUS-partner shelter to needlessly kill virtually every animal in its facility, HSUS did not condemn the action or support activists working to end such practices. HSUS defended the shelter, arguing that the killing was legitimate and proper. More than 170 dogs and cats lay dead, the victims of a senseless slaughter by inept and uncaring shelter management. A former shelter employee says she'll never forget the image: "They were all piled on top of each other, just lying there dead." These actions by HSUS mirror those they have taken in Wilkes County, North Carolina, Eugene, Oregon, King County, Washington, Randolph, Iowa, Paige County, Virginia, New York City and elsewhere—defending kill-oriented shelters while undermining No Kill reform efforts.

Yet, ironically, in campaigning for Proposition 2, HSUS argued that since people would not treat pets the way animals in factory farms are treated (an acknowledgment of the American public's deep concern for dogs and cats), they shouldn't allow chickens, pigs, and calves to be treated in such a manner. "We wouldn't force our pets to live in cramped cages," argued supporters. "All animals, including those raised for food, deserve humane treatment."

But that is exactly how dogs and cats are treated in the very shelters that HSUS champions, and their mass killing is the ultimate expression of inhumane treatment. In fact, HSUS is the primary architect of the paradigm that says killing animals in shelters is an act of kindness and the originators of the abominable euphemism "putting them to sleep," which Bonnie Silva, in her book *Fifteen Legs*, states "cannot provide a thick enough gloss to conceal the disturbing, awful truth." While current leadership at HSUS has stated that focusing on farmed animals is a top priority, the focus is not mutually exclusive with a campaign for a No Kill nation. The push toward No Kill would not detract from their focus on farmed animals and would, in fact, further that cause by setting a precedent regarding the sanctity of animal life. Moreover, in light of our knowledge and ability to end the killing, HSUS cannot ignore its duty to overturn the deadly paradigm that it created and that has directly resulted in the potential for being killed faced by every animal that enters a U.S. shelter today.

Over forty years ago, HSUS championed a philosophy that excused killing, often promoted it, and cemented its hegemony, all at the expense of the animals. Their historical and present statements—including the myths of pet overpopulation, that no one wants to kill, that killing is the public's fault, that killing is kindness, and that shelters can only adopt a precious few and kill the rest—have all been proven false yet have rationalized an infrastructure responsible for the continued mass extermination of dogs and cats.

When HSUS leadership accepted their positions, they also accepted the responsibility to right those wrongs. Specifically, it is their duty to redirect HSUS' Companion Animal division, which has enormous authority and influence over how shelters in this country operate, to champion life instead of death.

WHERE DO WE GO FROM HERE?

We know how to end the killing. Over the past five years, many animal control shelters across the United States have embraced not only the No Kill philosophy, but the programs and services that make it possible. As a result, they are achieving unprecedented lifesaving success, saving more than 90 percent of animals. Death rates are plummeting and adoptions are skyrocketing in these communities, and these results have been achieved virtually overnight, proving that saving lives is less a function of any perceived pet overpopulation, but rather of a shelter's leadership and practices.

In the history of animal protection, this news is seminal, as it harkens the fulfillment of the chief goal of the No Kill movement—ending the killing of savable animals in U.S. shelters. The formula for saving the lives of four million dogs and cats, and hundreds of thousands of other animals, has been discovered. And groups like HSUS should work feverishly to ensure that this formula is replicated in every community across the country.

Sadly, they are not. But we need not wait for them to lead us. Instead, we must lead them. The public is already on our side and calling for a change in the status quo. We're the ones we've been waiting for. We have found our voice, and recognize the potential its fullest expression can create. *No more compromises. No more killing.*

We're on the Same Team

I BELIEVE that dogs, cats and other companion animals in U.S. shelters have a right to live. I also believe that some day that right will be absolute as the shelter reform movement dovetails with the animal sanctuary and hospice care movements. At this time in history, however, the initial goal is to provide a lifesaving guarantee for those animals who are healthy and treatable. In other words, the No Kill movement is trying to save the roughly 95 percent of shelter animals who are not hopelessly ill or injured, irremediably suffering, or vicious dogs with a poor prognosis for rehabilitation.

Some, perhaps most, No Kill advocates would never use the word "rights" to describe what they seek for sheltered animals, and in fact, have a deep and almost unbending bias against the concept of "animal rights." They view the animal rights movement with suspicion because they believe it is epitomized by People for the Ethical Treatment of Animals. PETA has embraced systematic killing of animals in shelters, supports punitive laws that harm animals, and kills animals itself—roughly 2,000 a year, over 90 percent of all animals they take in. In addition, Ingrid Newkirk, PETA's founder, has publicly embraced campaigns to exterminate Pit Bulls in shelters, opposed non-lethal solutions for feral cats, and called killing a "gift" for the animals, even in the face of readily available lifesaving alternatives.

In reality, PETA's viewpoint does not reflect the animal rights philosophy. But because other animal rights groups and some animal rights activists do not challenge PETA (and, in some cases, embrace it), the belief that it does is understandable. In truth, the No Kill philosophy lies at the intersection of the movement for animal rights and the one that calls itself the "animal welfare" movement. In other words, the No Kill movement shares a great deal with the animal rights movement as it relates to companion animals: both are seeking the right of the animals to live. We saw this common ground recently when an online discussion group dedicated to animal rights, found itself at the center of the PETA killing controversy. In 2008, PETA killed 555 of the 584 dogs and 1,569 of the 1,589 cats it sought out. Despite $30 million in annual revenues and millions of animal-loving members, it claimed it could only find homes for seven out of 2,216 animals. After members of the animal rights online discussion group condemned PETA, PETA posted a defense of its actions. In response, leadership of the group removed PETA's posting privileges. In kicking PETA out of the group, they stated:

> The AR in [our name] is Animal Rights. No animal needs the 'right' to be killed. Yes, there are concerns about the way some no-kill shelters operate, and these need to be dealt with accordingly—but to lump them all together and to oppose no-kill entirely is wrongminded, dishonest and in opposition to animal rights. Let me be clear: the advocacy of killing healthy animals will NOT be tolerated.

This is exciting news—news the No Kill movement should celebrate. Because of the opening this action provides, I am making a plea for unity between what activists within these movements mistakenly see as two opposing camps on the issue of companion animals. I make this plea to my fellow No Kill advocates, who focus their advocacy for dogs and cats on ending their killing in shelters and protecting their relationship with their own companion animals, a relationship as strong as family. I also make this plea to my colleagues in the animal rights movement, who should see the fight for a No Kill nation as a worthy goal consistent with their larger beliefs. On this score, we have common ground. On the issue of dogs and cats, we can no longer afford to be a divided movement; the division is hurting our ability to achieve success.

Regardless of how many blogs and articles about PETA's hypocrisy are written, they do nothing to stop the people at PETA from killing. These articles do nothing to give them pause, and will continue to do nothing, because PETA is immune to bad press or condemnation from outside the animal rights movement. Were the pressure from within the movement itself to increase, were more organizations to do what the online discussion group did and reject PETA's leadership, were other leaders in the animal rights movement to feel the heat from the embrace of, association with, and celebration of PETA, were newspapers to earnestly discuss PETA's position on companion animals not as an "official" animal rights position but as the singular, bizarre, irresponsible, and cruel views of one group shunned by other animal rights organizations, PETA would lose any legitimacy it currently has with the media and the public. But right now, we—No Kill advocates and animal rights activists—only give them power by squabbling over issues extraneous to this discussion and focusing on our differences rather than our significant commonalities on the issue of saving companion animals in shelters.

Today, PETA will likely kill animals. Tomorrow, some family may surrender their dog to PETA, falsely believing that the animal will find a good home only to have the pet killed at PETA's Norfolk, Virginia facility or even in the back of a van, as PETA has admitted doing. PETA statistics show that such a scenario may occur five times a day, every day of the year. We must stop merely talking about this. We must end it.

But instead of working with their animal rights counterparts, No Kill advocates are suspicious of them. Mention the words "animal rights," and most in the No Kill movement run for cover. They think that because they don't subscribe to the rest of the ideals of the animal rights movement, they must reject all of it. They think animal rights groups are trying to abolish sharing one's home with animal companions. And they think of mass killing in shelters. As a result, they oppose anything that smacks of giving animals "rights" and belittle it as something to be shunned and avoided at all possible costs. This view is counterproductive.

The goal of every social movement is legislation to gain and then protect the rights of its members or the focus of its efforts, and the No Kill movement must stop acting like it is the exception. The suffrage movement wasn't just seeking discretionary permission from elections officials to vote, an ability that could be taken away. Its goal was winning the *right* to vote, a right guaranteed in law. The civil rights movement wasn't just seeking the discretionary ability to sit at the front of the bus or to eat at the same lunch counters (and so much more). Its goal was winning the *right* to do so, a right guaranteed in law. The movement for marriage equality isn't just seeking the discretionary opportunity to marry despite sexual orientation. Its goal is winning the *right* to do so, a right guaranteed in law. Because without legal rights, one's fate is contingent on who the election official is, who the restaurant owner is, and who the mayor is. And just as quickly as permission is given, it can be taken away.

In the sheltering context, I have long called for regime change, for the removal of shelter directors who find it easier to end life than to save life. But just replacing them with leadership passionate about saving lives and committed to implementing the programs and services of the No Kill Equation is ultimately not enough. The next director who comes along has unlimited discretion and can choose to reverse that success. A system that gives power to one person to say "Yes" to No Kill also creates the power of one person to thwart it. In the end, no group—including shelter animals—is safe in a legal republic without the rights afforded by law.

Laws codify norms of behavior and, at their best, help create a just and thoughtful society. We have—and embrace—voting rights acts, environmental protection laws, and laws against discrimination based on gender, race, and sexual orientation. Ultimately, such laws are essential to ensure that fair and equal treatment is guaranteed, not subject to the discretion of those in power. We shouldn't just want a promise that shelters will try to do better. We already have such promises—and millions of animals are still being killed. We must demand accountability beyond the rhetoric. And we shouldn't simply be seeking progressive directors willing to save lives. We should demand that the killing end, now and forever, regardless of who is running the shelters. And we get that in only one way: *by passing legislation that gives sheltered animals the right to live.*

But too many dog and cat lovers have abandoned this goal for the No Kill movement. While they embrace No Kill and desire No Kill and even demand No Kill, they oppose giving dogs and cats legal "rights." They resist the very thing that is essential to creating and sustaining a No Kill nation. They rally against what they should be seeking; fighting it, they inadvertently undermine that which they claim they want. And the longer they reject this vital tool in building the legal infrastructure for success, the harder and more protracted they make the struggle to achieve the goal.

As I noted above, these individuals and groups attack the concept of rights because they believe that the term "animal rights" means the end of sharing one's life and home with a companion animal, and it means mass slaughter of dogs and cats. In short, that it means PETA. But PETA is not an "animal rights" group.

The right to life is universally acknowledged as basic or fundamental. It is basic or fundamental because the enjoyment of the right to life is a necessary condition of the enjoyment of all other rights. A movement cannot be "rights" oriented, as PETA claims to be, yet ignore the right to life. If an animal is dead, the animal's rights are irrelevant. Not only does PETA not acknowledge the right to life, it has rejected it; PETA's leader Ingrid Newkirk says she "does not believe in right to life." And the organization acts upon that position by seeking out and killing 2,000 animals every year.

And not only is PETA not an animal rights group, it is not an animal welfare organization or even an animal control agency. Its staff members kill in the face of lifesaving alternatives. And its record of killing puts it even outside the purview of an animal control orientation, except in the most regressive of agencies that do not make any animals available for adoption. Indeed, there is no philosophical foundation for the belief that animals should be sought out and killed.

Such a philosophy is not rational. It is not compassionate or ethical. It will never have widespread appeal. It does not represent what animal rights activists want for companion animals. And when this ugly, tragic chapter in the movement's history finally ends, when PETA can no longer intimidate those who challenge the killing or have witnessed first hand the grisly reality behind their locked doors, when those people come forward, and when we finally have the whole, gruesome truth set before us as to what PETA has been doing to animals at their facility for the last decade, there will be no animal rights groups championing or defending PETA.

What drives this continued association and cooperation with PETA within the animal rights movement is not a shared vision but rather simple cowardice and indifference. It is not an agreement with the principles or the extermination campaign. Currently, PETA threatens legal action against those who criticize the killing. But as more voices bravely reject the killing, it will embolden others to do the same. Activists and animal rights organizations are afraid to challenge PETA, and their silence—their complicity—gives an impression that they agree with the platform. Ultimately, PETA gets its power from the silence of these groups and by activists. Were there to be a united front against PETA's dark and nefarious agenda within the animal rights movement, their power would dwindle and ultimately disappear.

And while some in the No Kill movement might be tempted to view the support PETA receives from some animal rights activists as proof of their embrace of PETA's views, it would be a mistake to assume that such people actually endorse a campaign of extermination. They are, instead, under the sway of the dishonest rhetoric that justifies the bloodshed. In other words, they are not defending PETA as a rational reflection of their beliefs; they do so because PETA misleads them. Leadership at PETA knows that a campaign for animal extermination would gain very few followers. And though PETA's killing has absolutely nothing to do with sheltering, they make the killing more publicly palatable by packing it in the false dogmas that have been used for decades to justify shelter killing.

First, they say they have no choice but to kill because of pet overpopulation, the same myth used to justify killing in shelters across the country. Second, they tell activists that all the animals PETA kills are irremediably suffering, a claim contradicted by sworn testimony in court by a veterinarian and others. In addition, Newkirk herself has admitted

they kill healthy, adoptable animals. Third, they claim that all controversy about their killing is being manipulated by industries that exploit
animals and people who want to destroy the animal rights movement: a
classic case of "if you can't argue with the message, attack the messenger." Lacking a more sophisticated and educated understanding of No
Kill, and possessing a misplaced trust in PETA, some animal rights activists rally to their defense because they believe PETA—not because they
believe that dogs and cats should be slaughtered.

Admittedly, there are some activists who actually know that PETA
kills animals in the face of alternatives and have defended it with varia-
tions of the argument "they do so much other good for animals" or "they
have seen more pain and suffering than we can ever know." This view
is obviously flawed and definitely tragic in its Orwellian forgiveness
of the killing. Whatever else PETA does for animals or however much
suffering PETA staff claim to have seen is irrelevant; nothing gives the
group a blank check to cause even more harm by killing animals. And,
of course, this argument ignores that it is not *who* is right that must be
defended, but *what* is right. But here again, it is not about any cogent
philosophy of "animal rights." People who embrace PETA—despite
awareness of the mass killing—aren't motivated by belief that dogs and
cats should be killed because sharing one's home with companion animals is evil. Instead, they are driven by self-regard, setting themselves
up as "better" because they oppose the "uncaring masses." And even
when PETA acts in contradiction to the principles of animal rights,
their allegiance remains with the institution because "I'm with PETA"
has a social connotation of being radical that makes them special, and
therefore distinct from the rest of us. For these people, it isn't and never has been about the animals but about themselves; it isn't about what
they can do to help animals, but about what their association with PETA
gives them—*an identity.*

There is no animal rights agenda to exterminate dogs and cats. And
there is no animal rights agenda to make it illegal to share one's home
and one's life with dogs and cats. Most animal rights activists share their
own homes with animal companions. It would make no sense for them to
believe chickens, cows, pigs, and other animals have a right to live, but

dogs and cats should be killed. That is a *non-sequitur* that cannot be as-
cribed to the movement as a whole. Yet even if there were such an agenda,
there would never be a critical consensus favoring such an approach and
therefore no shift in the national consciousness to bring victory for such
a bizarre scheme.

Predicated upon the extermination of beings most Americans consider cherished family members, PETA's repugnant agenda inspires in
the No Kill movement a fear of contagion that is disproportionate to its
actual threat. And to allow such overstated fear to drive a corrosive wedge
between No Kill advocates and animal rights activists sustains, rather
than hinders, the deadly actions of PETA, as well as that organization's
opposition to the No Kill movement.

In fact, the goals of the animal rights movement are in line with those
of No Kill. Many of the excuses that animal rights activists use to defend
PETA or to push for counterproductive, punitive laws were dogmas advanced by many in the shelter reform movement until very recently—the
myths of pet overpopulation and that animals must be killed because
people don't care enough. No Kill advocates must help animal rights
activists move beyond these antiquated, harmful, and disproven false-
hoods as they freed themselves. Imagine what could be accomplished If
these two groups came together around the goals they share. The voices
championing No Kill would increase exponentially.

Ultimately, we all seek to end the senseless killing of animals in
shelters—especially those animals not suffering. Although a lot of people
do not use the term, what the No Kill movement advocates is for sheltered
animals to be given the *right* to live. And the reason many in the No Kill
movement do not talk that way, or make it a part of their overall strategy,
is because PETA has hijacked the term "animal rights."

Moreover, even if people continue to believe that the animal rights
agenda includes an end to companion animals through their extermination, the way to stop that "agenda" would be to outlaw it, to give animals
the rights that protect them. By embracing the right to life for dogs and
cats in shelters, and by passing legislation making it illegal to kill dogs and
cats, No Kill advocates would destroy what they see as the "animal rights
agenda." It makes no sense to respond to PETA's anti-animal position by

embracing a response that is also anti-animal and that supports—rather than challenges—PETA's position.

We end the killing of savable companion animals by taking away people's discretion to kill them. If we allow ourselves to reject rights in law for dogs and cats, then we are allowing the triumph of a position antithetical to everything both the No Kill and animal rights movements stand for. This includes rights that would prevent inhumane conditions and wholesale slaughter that animals currently face in too many communities. That is our common goal, our common belief, and thus our common ground. And with that common ground *on the issue of saving dogs and cats*, we also have a common enemy: PETA.

Neither the No Kill movement nor the larger animal rights movement can afford to allow the public to perceive PETA as a legitimate representative of the animal rights movement on the issue of companion animals; doing so gives them stature which they abuse to the detriment of animals—sowing seeds of doubt and confusion about the viability and desirability of No Kill.

Among the public and the media, there is the erroneous perception that PETA represents the most progressive voice on animal protection. Because No Kill advocates reject "animal rights," they are perceived as less progressive. In the public debate about who is the most pro-animal, nuanced analysis is often lost, so PETA's view carries the day. If the most "radical" animal rights group says No Kill is a sham and killing animals is both necessary and proper, people conclude it must be true. After all, they are PETA! No Kill advocates must no longer allow this.

The term "animal rights" is not going away, and it shouldn't. It is a term intended to put the movement in line with other social justice movements—to build on other rights-based movements and the philosophies they rest on. It is a powerful term encapsulating what the No Kill movement seeks for dogs and cats. And, when it comes to these animals, the public is ready and willing to embrace it. The No Kill movement is the nation's most progressive voice for companion animal rights. By rejecting the mantle that is rightfully ours, No Kill advocates inadvertently cede the moral high ground to those who use it to justify killing.

Having said that, animal rights activists must also be taken to task for not condemning PETA's killing. No other movement would allow someone like Newkirk to remain in her position without a massive outcry and public condemnation when their actions are so contrary to their movement's foremost principles. The child protection movement would not allow someone who kills children to run a children's rights organization. The human rights movement would not allow someone who kills people to run any of their organizations. But the animal rights movement—a movement founded on the principle that animals have a right to life— allows a killer of animals to run an animal rights organization. And with the exception of Friends of Animals, the rest of the nation's animal rights groups remain deafeningly silent about it.

Moreover, the lack of real understanding in the animal rights movement about No Kill allows for the ongoing embrace of programs that harm animals and perpetuates the false notion that No Kill means warehousing animals. Those in the animal rights movement must realize that it is shelters themselves, not the public, that are to blame for the killing in shelters and target their advocacy accordingly. They must reject the double standard that advocates a right to live for other animals but defends the killing of dogs and cats in shelters. They must educate themselves that the historical animosity to No Kill in the animal rights movement is not based upon any coherent philosophy but arises from the simple fact that some of the leaders of these organizations, such as Ingrid Newkirk, worked at shelters that killed animals. In fact, many of them killed thousands of animals themselves. This fact is the sole cause of the double standard between companion animals and all others.

Finally, although rescuers and some No Kill advocates may not embrace the animal rights platform in its entirety, dismissing No Kill and No Kill advocates on this point is harmful to animals and short-sighted— as it ignores an incredible opportunity to work together to realize the tremendous lifesaving the No Kill movement offers. Animal rights activists must appreciate that there are millions of animals alive today who owe their lives to the tireless work of people in the No Kill movement who share their love of dogs and cats and actively demonstrate that devotion through hard work—people who spend their money and time rescuing animals from death row at regressive shelters; people who spend their nights bottle-feeding orphaned kittens and puppies; people who provide care for homeless animals day in and day out. They would recognize that on the issue of dogs and cats, these individuals deserve gratitude for their noble, tireless, and selfless efforts; that they don't want dogs and cats killed just as animal rights activists don't want cows, chickens, or pigs to be killed. In recognizing this, animal rights activists would stop perpetuating overly simplistic ideas about who is "good" and who is "bad" in our relationship with animal companions.

In doing so, animal rights advocates would come to appreciate that just because some No Kill advocates don't share *all* of their goals, it does not follow that they are not legitimate agents to work for rights for dogs and cats. Movements can seek redress for social ills one at a time. And groups can come together to do so, even when they disagree about a larger platform. Moreover, if animal rights activists build trust by working with No Kill advocates on this issue, they will have formed a relationship which can be used to introduce them to larger animal rights issues.

Without disagreement and dissent, a movement stagnates and becomes ineffective. Dissent—when it challenges the status quo by revealing hypocrisy—is essential for progress. But internal dissent based on false premises and misunderstandings can be toxic to a movement, senselessly dividing those who should be united, and dwindling the power and efficacy of all parties by diverting attention and energy from the mission and from the fight against their common enemies.

When the online discussion group kicked PETA off of its list and took away its ability to post comments on the website, the group stated,

> PETA claims to be an animal rights group. Why would any animal demand the right to be murdered by their supposed rescuer and advocates? Can you imagine Amnesty International or the United Nations demanding that a population of humans be killed because they don't want to bother finding any food or shelter for them? PETA is not an animal rights group, in any meaningful sense of the term. It's disgusting and perverse that PETA is working so hard to derail the no-kill movement... Who needs an 'advocate' like that?

Some No Kill advocates may not agree with the entire animal rights platform, but how could they disagree with that? Common ground. A common goal. And a common enemy. We are allies on this one. And we need to work together to further the legal rights of dogs and cats in shelters because in doing so, we can finally and permanently stop not only PETA's campaign of killing, but their campaign to derail No Kill initiatives nationwide.

No Kill in a Nutshell

- Follow the Sodium Pentobarbital: the more shelters use, the more they will parrot untrue clichés about the "need" to kill, and the more they will lie about why they kill.
- Get the facts before you believe something and accept it as true, such as the existence of "pet overpopulation," simply because others believe it.
- Blanket statements about the existence of pet overpopulation ("there is pet overpopulation") are not facts, no matter how often they are repeated, no matter how many people repeat them.
- No one—not a single, solitary person—would believe that "killing is kindness" if they were facing the needle.
- Communities of every demographic (north, south, urban, rural, public animal control shelter, private shelter) have achieved No Kill success.
- Yes, we *can* adopt our way out of killing.
- The biggest variables in whether or not animals live or die are the choices made by shelter leadership.

- Traditional (regressive, kill-oriented) shelter policies are at odds with American humane values.
- The first step to No Kill is replacing kill-oriented directors.
- Feral cats are not homeless. Their home is outdoors and they have flourished outdoors for 10,000 years. Their habitat must be respected and their needs must be accommodated.
- The goal is not no more feral cats or no more homeless animals, as there will always be feral cats and a need for shelters for animals who become lost or lose their caretakers. The goal is no more *killing* of these animals.
- Five-and ten-year No Kill plans are ploys to diffuse criticism and delay accountability. A sincere commitment to No Kill by shelter and community leadership can result in virtually overnight success.
- Even if we (wrongly) assume we can never cross the goal line of No Kill success, we will still save millions of lives just by trying. That is worth doing and worth doing today.

Appendix I:

The Declaration of the No Kill Movement in the United States

THIS YEAR, SOME four million dogs and cats will be killed in shelters. The vast majority can and should be placed into loving homes or should never enter shelters in the first place. But there is hope.

No Kill sheltering models, based on innovative, non-lethal programs and services, have already saved the lives of millions of animals. But instead of embracing No Kill, many shelters—and their national agency allies—cling to their failed models of the past, models that result in the killing of millions of dogs and cats in U.S. shelters every year.

No Kill is a revolution. And behind every revolution is a declaration—a statement of grievances, and a listing of rights and principles that underscore our great hope for the future. We assert that a No Kill nation is within our reach—that the killing can and should be brought to an end.

I. PREAMBLE

One hundred and fifty years ago, societies for the prevention of cruelty to animals and other humane organizations were founded to establish standards for humane treatment of animals, to promote their rights, and to protect them from harm. This marked the formal beginning of the humane movement in the United States.

The scope and influence of these early humane organizations were testament to the public's concern for animals. It did not take long for them to set their sights on the abuse of homeless animals and cruel methods of killing by public pounds. It was common practice at the time for city and town dogcatchers to beat, drown, or shoot homeless animals.

Many humane agencies responded by entering into animal control contracts with towns and cities to ensure that the killing was done more humanely. But in taking on municipal animal control duties, these agencies abandoned their lifesaving and life-enhancing platforms when those beliefs conflicted with their contractual responsibilities. In the current era, where laws require killing by even more "humane" methods, these contradictions have become starker.

Increasingly, the practices of both humane societies and municipal animal control agencies are out of step with public sentiment. Today, most Americans hold the humane treatment of animals as a personal value, which is reflected in our laws, cultural practices, the proliferation of organizations founded for animal protection, increased per capita spending on animal care, and great advancements in veterinary medicine. But the agencies that the public expects to protect animals are instead killing four million animals annually.

Lifesaving alternatives to the mass killing of animals in shelters have existed for decades. These lifesaving methods are based on innovative, humane, nonlethal programs and services that have proven that the killing can be brought to an end. Too many of these agencies, however, remain mired in the kill philosophies of the past, unwilling to or hampered from exploring and adopting methods that save lives. This is a breach of their public trust, a gross deviation from their responsibility to protect animals, and a point of view that we, as caring people and a humane community, can no longer accept or tolerate.

We assert that a No Kill nation is within our reach—that the killing can and must be brought to an end. It is up to each of us working individually and together to implement sheltering models that have already saved tens of thousands of animals in progressive communities. If we work together—with certainty of purpose, assured of our own success, with the commitment that "what must be done, will be done"—the attainment of our goals will not be far off.

II. NO KILL RESOLUTION

Whereas, the right to live is every animal's most basic and fundamental right;

Whereas, societies for the prevention of cruelty to animals and other humane organizations were founded to establish standards for humane treatment of animals, to promote their rights, and to protect them from harm;

Whereas, traditional sheltering practices allow the mass killing of sheltered animals;

Whereas, every year shelters in the United States are killing millions of healthy and treatable animals who could be placed in homes, and are also killing millions of feral cats who do not belong in shelters;

Whereas, life always takes precedence over expediency;

Whereas, the No Kill movement in the United States has successfully implemented new and innovative programs that provide alternatives to mass killing;

Whereas, lifesaving change will come about only if No Kill programs are embraced and further developed;

Whereas, failure to implement No Kill programs constitutes a breach of the public's trust in the sheltering community;

Now, therefore, be it resolved that No Kill policies and procedures are the only legitimate foundation for animal sheltering; and,

It is incumbent upon all shelters and animal groups to embrace the philosophy of No Kill, to immediately begin implementing programs and services that will end the mass killing of sheltered animals, and to reject the failed kill-oriented practices of the past.

III. STATEMENT OF RIGHTS

We acknowledge the following:

- Sheltered animals have a right to live;
- Feral cats have a right to their lives and their habitats;

- Animals, rescuers, and the public have a right to expect animal protection organizations and animal shelters to do everything in their power to promote, protect, and advocate for the lives of animals;
- Animal protection groups, rescue groups, and No Kill shelters have a right to take into their custody animals who would otherwise be killed by animal shelters;
- Taxpayers and community members have a right to have their government spend tax monies on programs and services whose purpose is to save and enhance the lives of all animals;
- Taxpayers and community members have a right to full and complete disclosure about how animal shelters operate.

IV. GUIDING PRINCIPLES

No Kill is achieved only by guaranteeing the following:

- Life to all healthy animals, and to all sick, injured, or vicious animals where medical or behavioral intervention would alter a poor or grave prognosis;
- The right of feral cats to live in their habitats.

These conditions can be achieved only through adherence to the following:

- Shelters and humane groups end the killing of healthy and treatable animals, including feral cats;
- Every animal in a shelter receives individual consideration, regardless of how many animals a shelter takes in, or whether such animals are healthy, underaged, elderly, sick, injured, traumatized, or feral;
- Shelters and humane organizations discontinue the use of language that misleads the public and glosses over the nature of their actions, such as "euthanasia," "unadoptable," "fractious," "putting them to sleep," and other euphemisms that downplay the gravity of ending life and make the task of killing easier;

- Shelters are open to the public during hours that permit working people to reclaim or adopt animals during nonworking hours;
- Shelters and other government agencies promote spay/neuter programs and mandate that animals be spayed or neutered before adoption;
- Public shelters work with humane animal adoption organizations to the fullest extent to promote the adoption of animals and to reduce the rate of killing;
- Shelters provide care and treatment for all animals in shelters to the extent necessary, including prompt veterinary care, adequate nutrition, shelter, exercise, and socialization;
- Shelters are held accountable for and make information publicly available about all the animals in their care.

V. NO KILL STANDARDS

The implementation of these lifesaving procedures, policies, and programs must be the immediate goal of every shelter, and animal control and animal welfare agency:

- Formal, active commitment by shelter directors, management, and staff to lifesaving programs and policies, and dedication to promptly ending mass killing of shelter animals;
- Immediate implementation of the following programs by all publicly funded or subsidized animal shelters:
  - *High-volume, low-and no-cost spay/neuter services;*
  - *A foster care network for underaged, traumatized, sick, injured, or other animals needing refuge before any sheltered animal is killed, unless the prognosis for rehabilitation of that individual animal is poor or grave;*
  - *Comprehensive adoption programs that operate during weekend and evening hours and include offsite adoption venues;*
  - *Medical and behavioral rehabilitation programs;*
  - *Pet retention programs to solve medical, environmental, or behavioral problems and keep animals with their caring and responsible caregivers;*

- *Trap-Neuter-Return or Release (TNR) programs;*
- *Rescue group access to shelter animals;*
- *Volunteer programs to socialize animals, promote adoptions, and help in the operations of the shelter;*
- *Documentation before any animal is killed that all efforts to save the animal have been considered, including medical and behavioral rehabilitation, foster care, rescue groups, neuter and release, and adoption.*

- An end to the policy of accepting trapped feral cats to be destroyed as unadoptable, and implementation of TNR as the accepted method of feral cat control by educating the public about TNR and offering TNR program services;
- An end to the use of temperament testing that results in killing animals who are not truly vicious (e.g., shy/timid cats and frightened dogs) but who can be placed in homes, or are feral cats who can be returned or released;
- Abolishment of trapping, lending traps to the public to capture animals, and support of trapping by shelters, governments, and pest control companies for the purposes of removing animals to be killed;
- An end to owner-requested killing of animals unless the shelter has made an independent determination that the animal is irremediably suffering or cannot be rehabilitated;
- The repeal of unenforceable and counter-productive animal control ordinances such as cat licensing and leash laws, pet limit laws, bans on feeding stray animals, and bans on specific breeds.

Appendix II:
The No Kill Equation

Two DECADES AGO, the concept of a No Kill community was little more than a dream. Today, it is a reality in many cities and counties nationwide and the numbers continue to grow. And the first step is a decision, a commitment to reject kill-oriented ways of doing business. No Kill starts as an act of will.

Following a commitment to No Kill is the need for accountability. Accountability requires clear definitions, a lifesaving plan, and protocols and procedures oriented toward preserving life. But accountability also allows, indeed requires, flexibility. Too many shelters lose sight of this principle, staying rigid with shelter protocols, believing these are engraved in stone. They are not. Protocols are important because they ensure accountability from staff. But inflexible protocols can have the opposite effect: stifling innovation, causing lives to be needlessly lost, and allowing shelter employees who fail to save lives to hide behind a paper trail.

The decision to end an animal's life is extremely serious, and should always be treated as such. No matter how many animals a shelter kills, each and every animal is an individual, and each deserves individual consideration.

And finally, to meet the challenge that No Kill entails, shelter leadership needs to get the community excited, to energize people for the task at hand. By working with people, implementing lifesaving programs, and treating each life as precious, a shelter can transform a community.

The mandatory programs and services include:

I. Feral Cat TNR Program. Trap-Neuter-Release (TNR) programs allow shelters to reduce death rates.

II. High-Volume, Low-Cost Spay/Neuter. No- and low-cost, high-volume spay/neuter reduces the number of animals entering the shelter system, allowing more resources to be allocated toward saving lives.

III. Rescue Groups. An adoption or transfer to a rescue group frees up scarce cage and kennel space, reduces expenses for feeding, cleaning, killing, and improves a community's rate of lifesaving. Because millions of dogs and cats are killed in shelters annually, rare is the circumstance in which a rescue group should be denied an animal.

IV. Foster Care. Volunteer foster care is a low-cost, and often no-cost way of increasing a shelter's capacity, caring for sick and injured or behaviorally challenged animals, and thus saving more lives.

V. Comprehensive Adoption Programs. Adoptions are vital to an agency's lifesaving mission. The quantity and quality of shelter adoptions is in shelter management's hands, making lifesaving a direct function of shelter policies and practice. If shelters better promoted their animals and had adoption programs responsive to community needs, including public access hours for working people, offsite adoptions, adoption incentives, and effective marketing, they could increase the number of homes available and replace killing with adoptions. Contrary to conventional wisdom, shelters can adopt their way out of killing.

VI. Pet Retention. While some surrenders of animals to shelters are unavoidable, others can be prevented—but only if shelters work with people to help them solve their problems. Saving animals requires shelters to develop innovative strategies for keeping people and their companion animals together. And the more a community sees its shelters as a place to turn for advice and assistance, the easier this job will be.

VII. Medical and Behavior Programs. To meet its commitment to a life-saving guarantee for all savable animals, shelters need to keep animals happy and healthy and keep animals moving efficiently through the system. To do this, shelters must put in place comprehensive vaccination, handling, cleaning, socialization, and care policies before animals get sick and rehabilitative efforts for those who come in sick, injured, un-weaned, or traumatized.

VIII. Public Relations/Community Involvement. Increasing adoptions, maximizing donations, recruiting volunteers and partnering with community agencies comes down to increasing the shelter's public exposure. And that means consistent marketing and public relations. Public relations and marketing are the foundation of a shelter's activities and success.

IX. Volunteers. Volunteers are a dedicated "army of compassion" and the backbone of a successful No Kill effort. There is never enough staff, never enough dollars to hire more staff, and always more needs than paid human resources. That is where volunteers make the difference between success and failure and, for the animals, life and death.

X. Proactive Redemptions. One of the most overlooked areas for reducing killing in animal control shelters are lost animal reclaims. Shifting from a passive to a more proactive approach has allowed shelters to return a large percentage of lost animals to their families.

XI. A Compassionate Director. The final element of the No Kill Equation is the most important of all, without which all other elements are thwarted—a hard working, compassionate animal control or shelter director not content to continue killing, while regurgitating tired clichés about "public irresponsibility" or hiding behind the myth of "too many animals, not enough homes."

No Kill is simply not achievable without rigorous implementation of these programs. They provide the *only* model that ever created No Kill communities. It is up to us in the humane movement to demand them of our local shelters, and no longer to settle for the illusory excuses and smokescreens that shelters often put up in order to avoid implementing them.

COMPREHENSIVE IMPLEMENTATION

To fully succeed, however, shelters should not implement the programs piecemeal or in a limited manner. If they are sincere, animal shelters will implement and expand programs to the point that they replace killing entirely.

In 2004, for example, the Pennsylvania SPCA conducted fewer than 200 free spay/neuter surgeries for the pets of the community's low-income population. Shelter leaders can boast of a low-cost and free spay/neuter program, but 200 surgeries in a city of nearly 1.5 million people, with one in four of them below the federal poverty line, will not reduce the numbers of animals entering Philadelphia shelters. By contrast, the San Francisco SPCA, in a city with roughly half the population of Philadelphia, performed approximately 9,000 surgeries a year throughout the 1990s, roughly 80 percent of those were free.

Similarly, animal control in Austin, Texas allows only employees to participate in its foster care program. The shelter can claim to implement the programs and services of the No Kill Equation, but it excludes thousands of animal lovers from participating in the lifesaving effort, seriously limiting how many lives they save.

A shelter committed to No Kill does not send neonatal orphaned kittens into foster care "sometimes," but every time. A shelter committed to No Kill does not merely allow rescue groups access to animals "some of the time," but every time a legitimate rescue group is willing to take over care and custody of the animal. Indeed, a No Kill shelter actively seeks these groups out and contacts a particular rescue organization whenever an animal meets its criteria.

Shelters must also work harder to reunite lost animals with their families. Traditional shelters do little more than have people fill out lost pet reports. As a result, in a typical shelter, less than two percent of cats and roughly 20 percent of dogs are reclaimed. This is unfortunate because being more proactive and comprehensive would have a significant impact on lifesaving.

Those rare communities that have systematized their approach and become more proactive have more than doubled this rate of redemption. Washoe County Regional Animal Services in Reno, Nevada, for example, returned seven percent of lost cats and 60 percent of lost dogs to their homes in 2007. Given the high per capita intake of animals (which some suggest would evidence high rates of "public irresponsibility") one would expect the agency to have a very low redemption rate. Instead, it is very near the top in the nation. Why? The shelter is proactive in finding the people whose companion animals have become lost.

Before impounding stray dogs, Washoe County animal control officers check for identification, scan for microchips, knock on doors in the neighborhood where the animal was found, and talk to area residents. They also carry mobile telephones so that they can immediately call the missing animal's family and facilitate a quick reunion. While this may seem an obvious course of action, it is, unfortunately, uncommon in American shelters—tragically so. The more traditional approach is simply to impound any animals found wandering the streets and to transport them immediately to the pound. The animals get lost in the system, compete for kennel space with other animals, and are often put to death.

In Washoe County, impound is a last resort. But if animals are impounded, shelter staff is equally as proactive as field officers are in facilitating redemptions. They immediately post on the shelter's website photographs, identifying information, and the location of where the animal was found. People can search for the animals from their computers at home or at work.

These efforts in Washoe County, combined with an over 50 percent increase in the adoption rate in the community thanks to the Nevada Humane Society, has resulted in a 93 percent communitywide rate of shelter lifesaving for dogs and almost 90 percent for cats year-to-date in 2009. The difference between the average community and Washoe County is striking, but even more so because this latter community is still only scratching the surface. Some communities in the United States have achieved a nearly 65 percent reclaim rate for stray dogs; even higher rates have been achieved in other countries. The reclaim rate for cats can—and should—match these, rather than remain at deplorably low national averages.

This not only shows the achievement of a No Kill community is within our reach, it demonstrates how bringing shelters in line with the No Kill Equation can yield dramatic declines in killing virtually overnight.

In short, shelters must take killing off the table for savable animals, and utilize the programs and services of the No Kill Equation not some-times, not merely when it is convenient or politically expedient to do so, but *always*, for every single animal. A half-hearted effort isn't enough. It is primarily the shift from a reactive to proactive orientation and from a casual, ad-hoc, limited implementation to a comprehensive one that will lead to the greatest declines in killing, and fix our broken animal shelter system.

Appendix III:

The Companion Animal Protection Act

To ACHIEVE a No Kill nation, we must move beyond a system in which the lives of animals are subject to the discretion and whims of shelter leaders or health department bureaucrats. In a shelter reliant on killing, directors can come and go, the shelter continues killing, local government ignores the ongoing failure, and the public is told "there is no other way."

Meanwhile, No Kill is succeeding in communities where individual shelter leaders are committed to it by establishing the programs and services that make it possible. Unfortunately, such leaders are few and far between. When that leader leaves the organization, moreover, the vision can quickly be doomed. For No Kill success to be widespread and long lasting, we must move past a personality-based system and give shelter animals the rights and protections afforded by law.

Every successful social movement results in legal protections that codify expected policies and provide consequences for conduct that violates normative values. We need to regulate shelters in the same way we regulate hospitals and other agencies which hold the power over life and death.

The answer lies in passing and enforcing shelter reform legislation that mandates how all shelters must operate. The ideal animal control law would ban the killing of dogs and cats, and would prohibit the impounding of feral cats except for purposes of spay/neuter and release. But at this time in history, it is unlikely that local governments would pass such sweeping laws. The Companion Animal Protection Act (CAPA), therefore, was written as interim "model" legislation to maximize rates of lifesaving. No law can anticipate every contingency, and CAPA is no exception. It is not intended to be complete or to eliminate the need for other animal protection laws. Nor is it intended to reduce stronger protections that animals may have in a particular jurisdiction. The legislation can and should be modified in such circumstances.

But it is clear that too many shelters are not voluntarily implementing the programs and services that make No Kill possible. As a result, animals continue to be needlessly killed. In response, CAPA mandates these programs and services, follows the only model that has actually created No Kill communities, and focuses its efforts on the very shelters that are doing the killing. In this way, shelter leadership is forced to embrace No Kill and operate their shelters in a progressive, life-affirming way—removing the discretion which allows shelter leaders to ignore the best interests of the animals.

Companion Animal Protection Act Highlights:

- Establishes the shelter's primary role as saving the lives of animals
- Declares that saving lives and protecting public safety are compatible
- Establishes a definition of No Kill that includes all savable animals including feral cats
- Protects rabbits, birds, and other animals, as well as dogs and cats
- Makes it illegal for a shelter to kill an animal if a rescue group or No Kill shelter is willing to save that animal
- Requires shelters to provide animals with fresh food, fresh water, environmental enrichment, exercise, veterinary care, and cleanliness

- Requires shelters to have fully functioning adoption programs including offsite venues and the use of the internet to promote animals, and further mandates that shelters be open seven days per week for adoption
- Prohibits shelters from killing animals based on arbitrary criteria such as breed or when alternatives to killing exist
- Requires animal control to allow volunteers to help with fostering, socializing, and assisting with adoptions
- Requires shelters to be truthful about how many animals they kill and adopt and to report those statistics regularly
- Allows animal lovers to sue the shelter and compel compliance if shelters fail to do so

FULL TEXT OF THE COMPANION ANIMAL PROTECTION ACT

Part 1. Purpose and Intent.

SECTION 1(A) It is the intent of the City Council to end the killing of savable animals in the city. In order to accomplish this, the City Council finds and declares:

(1) protecting animals is a legitimate and compelling public interest; (2) the killing of savable animals in city shelters is a needless tragedy that must be brought to an end; (3) no animal should be killed if the animal can be placed in a suitable home, if a private sheltering agency or rescue group is willing to take care and custody of the animal for purposes of adoption, or, in the case of feral cats, if they can be sterilized and released to their habitats; (4) animals held in shelters deserve proper care and humane treatment including prompt veterinary care, adequate nutrition, shelter, exercise, environmental enrichment, and water; (5) shelters have a duty to make all savable animals available for adoption for a reasonable period of time;(6) owners of lost animals should have a reasonable period of time within which to redeem their animals;(7) shelters should not kill savable animals at the request of their owners; (8) all efforts should be made to encourage the voluntary spaying and neutering of animals;

(9) government is obligated to taxpayers and community members to spend tax monies on programs and services whose purpose is to save and enhance the lives of animals; (10) when animals are killed, it should be done as humanely and compassionately as possible; (11) taxpayers and community members deserve full and complete disclosure about how animal shelters operate;(12) citizens have a right to ensure that agencies follow the law; (13) saving the lives of animals, identifying and eliminating animal neglect and abuse, and protecting public safety are compatible interests; and, (14) policies that undermine the public's trust in animal shelters should be eliminated.

(B) The City Council further finds and declares that all public and private sheltering agencies that operate within the city shall:

(1) commit themselves to ending the killing of savable animals in their care and custody;(2) work with other animal adoption organizations to the fullest extent to promote the adoption of animals and to reduce the rate of killing; (3) provide every animal in their custody with individual consideration and care, regardless of how many animals they take in, or whether such animals are healthy, unweaned, elderly, sick, injured, traumatized, feral, aggressive, or of a particular breed;(4) not ban, bar, limit or otherwise obstruct the adoption of any animal based on arbitrary criteria, such as breed, age, color, or other criteria except as to the individual animal's medical condition or aggression, or the adopter's fitness to adopt.

(c) The City Council further finds and declares that all public sheltering agencies that operate within the city shall:

(1) be open to the public for adoption seven days per week;(2) implement programs to save lives, including free and low-cost spay/neuter services for animals, including feral cats; a foster-care network for animals needing special care, including unweaned, traumatized, sick and injured animals; comprehensive adoption programs that operate during weekend and evening hours and include adoption venues other than the shelter; medical and behavioral rehabilitation programs; pet-retention programs to solve medical, environmental, and behavioral problems and keep animals with their caring and responsible owners; and, volunteer programs to help

socialize animals, promote adoptions, and assist in the operations of the shelter.

(D) The City Council further finds and declares that ending the killing of savable animals will occur when all public and private sheltering agencies and rescue groups work together to achieve this goal, and therefore expects private sheltering agencies and rescue groups to:

(1) be open to the public during hours that permit working people to adopt animals during non-working hours;(2) implement programs to save lives, including free and low-cost spay/neuter services for animals, including feral cats; a foster-care network for animals needing special care, including unweaned, traumatized, sick and injured animals; comprehensive adoption programs that operate during weekend and evening hours and include adoption venues other than the shelter; medical and behavioral rehabilitation programs; pet-retention programs to solve medical, environmental, and behavioral problems and keep animals with their caring and responsible owners; and, volunteer programs to help socialize animals, promote adoptions, and assist in the operations of the shelter.

Part II. Definitions.

SEC. 2 (A) For purposes of this Act, the following defnitions shall apply: (1) a *Public Sheltering Agency* is a public animal control shelter or private shelter, society for the prevention of cruelty to animals, humane society, or animal adoption group that receives city funding and/or has a contract with the city under which it accepts stray or owner-relinquished animals. (2) a *Private Sheltering Agency* is a shelter, society for the prevention of cruelty to animals, humane society, or animal adoption group, which is designated as a non-profit under Section 501(c)(3) of the Internal Revenue Code, and: (a) which does not receive city funding or have a contract with the city under which it accepts stray or owner-relinquished animals; (b) accepts animals into a physical facility other than a private residence; and, (c) places into new homes stray and/or owner-relinquished animals and/or animals who have been removed from a public or private sheltering agency.

(3) a *Rescue Group* is a collaboration of individuals not operated for a profit, whose primary stated purpose is animal protection, which places into new homes stray and/or owner-relinquished animals and/or animals who have been removed from a public or private sheltering agency. Individual rescuers who keep animals in their own homes but are not part of a larger collaboration are not a rescue group for purposes of this Act. (4) an *Animal* is any domestic non-human living creature normally kept as a pet, or a feral cat. (5) an *Impounded* animal is any animal who enters a public or private sheltering agency or rescue group regardless of whether the animal is a stray, owner-relinquished, seized, taken into protective custody, transferred from another private or public sheltering agency, or is an animal whose owner requests that the animal be killed, except for any animal presented to a medical clinic associated with such agencies for purposes of preventative or rehabilitative medical care, or sterilization. (6) a *Stray* animal is any animal who is impounded without a known owner present at impound who is voluntarily relinquishing custody. (7) a *Savable* animal is any animal who is either healthy or treatable, and is not a vicious or dangerous dog. (8) a *Healthy* animal is any animal who is not sick or injured. (9) a *Treatable* animal is any animal who is sick or injured, whose prognosis for rehabilitation of that illness and/or injury is excellent, good, fair, or guarded as determined by a veterinarian licensed to practice in this state. (10) a *Non-rehabilitatable* animal is any animal with severe illness or injury whose prognosis for rehabilitation is either poor or grave as determined by a veterinarian licensed to practice in this state. (11) an *Irremediably Suffering* animal is any animal with a medical condition who has a poor or grave prognosis for being able to live without severe, unremitting pain, as determined by a veterinarian licensed to practice in this state. (12) a *Feral Cat* is a cat who is free-roaming, unsocialized to humans, and unowned. (13) a *Feral Cat Caregiver* is someone who cares for feral cats and has an interest in protecting the cats, but is not the owner of those cats. (14) an *Unweaned* animal is any neonatal animal who, in the absence of his/her mother, requires supplemental bottle feeding by humans in order to survive. In the case of puppies and kittens, unweaned animals are animals who fit the above description and are from 0 to 4 weeks of age. (15) a *Litter* of animals includes two or more animals

who are under twelve weeks of age as determined by a veterinarian licensed
to practice medicine in this state, or by a veterinary technician or veterinary assistant working under the direction of a veterinarian licensed to
practice medicine in this state. (16) a *Vicious Dog* is a dog who exhibits
aggression to people even when the dog is not hungry, in pain, or frightened, and whose prognosis for rehabilitation of that aggression is poor or
grave as determined by a trained behaviorist who is an expert on canine behavior. (17) a *Dangerous Dog* is a dog adjudicated to be vicious by a court of
competent jurisdiction and where all appeals of that judicial determination have been unsuccessful.

Part III. Sterilization Requirements.

SEC. 3(A) Except as otherwise provided in this section, no public or private sheltering agency or rescue group shall sell, adopt, or give away to a
new owner any dog, cat, rabbit, or other animal who has not been spayed
or neutered, except as follows:

(1) This section shall not apply to reptiles, amphibians, birds, fish, and small
animals such as mice and hamsters, where the anesthesia or sterilization
procedure is likely to result in the animal's death.

(B) If a veterinarian licensed to practice veterinary medicine in this state
certifies that an animal is too sick or injured to be spayed or neutered, or
that it would otherwise be detrimental to the health of the animal to be
spayed or neutered, the adopter or purchaser shall pay the public or private
sheltering agency or rescue group a deposit of not less than fifty dollars
($50), and not more than one hundred dollars ($100). This deposit shall
be returned if the adopter or purchaser presents the entity from which
the animal was obtained with proof that the animal has been spayed or
neutered within 60 days of receiving the animal, or presents a signed letter
from a veterinarian licensed to practice medicine in this state, certifying
that the animal has died, including a description of the animal and most
likely cause of death. This deposit shall also be returned upon the expiration the 60-day period if the adopter or purchaser presents a signed letter from a veterinarian licensed to practice medicine in this state, certifying

that upon the expiration of the 60-day period, the animal remains too sick or injured, or that it would otherwise be detrimental to the health of the animal, to be spayed or neutered.

(c) The adopter or purchaser of an animal must spay or neuter that animal within 60 days of adoption, purchase, or receipt from a public or private sheltering agency, or rescue group, except as follows:

(1) If a veterinarian licensed to practice medicine in this state certifies that an animal is too sick or injured or that it would otherwise be detrimental to the health of the animal to be spayed or neutered within the time period, such animal shall be spayed or neutered within 30 days of the veterinarian certifying that the animal may safely be spayed or neutered.

(D) Notwithstanding subsection (B), if a veterinarian licensed to practice medicine in this state certifies that an animal is too sick or injured to be spayed or neutered, or that it would otherwise be detrimental to the health of the animal to be spayed or neutered, and that the animal is not likely to ever be healthy enough to be spayed or neutered, no deposit shall be required.

(E) For purposes of this section, a determination that a dog or cat is too sick or injured to be spayed or neutered, or that it would otherwise be detrimental to his or her health, may not be made based solely on the youth of the dog or cat, so long as the dog or cat is at least eight weeks of age.

(F) Notwithstanding the other requirements of this section, animals may be transferred to organizations listed on the registry required under Section 9 before they have been spayed or neutered and without a spay/neuter deposit, as long as the receiving organization represents that it will spay or neuter all animals before placing them into homes.

(G) Any funds from unclaimed deposits made pursuant to this section shall be expended only for programs to spay or neuter animals.

(H) A licensed veterinarian shall perform spay/neuter operations under this Act.

SEC. 4(A) A person is subject to civil penalties of not less than two hundred dollars ($200) or more than five hundred dollars ($500) if that person does any of the following:(1) falsifies any proof of spaying or neutering submitted for the purpose of compliance with this Act;(2) intentionally issues a check for insufficient funds for any spaying or neutering deposit required under this Act; (3) falsifies a signed letter from a veterinarian submitted for the purpose of compliance with this Act, certifying that an animal is too sick or injured to be spayed or neutered;(4) fails to sterilize the animal as required.

(B) An action for a penalty proposed under this section may be commenced in a court of competent jurisdiction by the administrator of the public or private animal sheltering agency or rescue group from which the recipient obtained the animal who is the subject of the violation.

(c) All penalties collected under this section shall be retained by the agency bringing the action under subsection (B) to be used solely for programs to spay or neuter animals.

Part IV. Feral Cats.

SEC. 5(A) Caretakers of feral cats shall be exempted from any provision of law proscribing the feeding of stray animals, requiring permits for the feeding of animals, requiring the confinement of cats, or limiting the number of animals a person can own, harbor, or have custody of, except as follows:(1) Nothing in this section shall be construed to limit the enforcement of a statute having as its effect the prevention or punishment of animal neglect or cruelty, so long as such enforcement is based on the conditions of animals, and not based on the mere fact that a person is feeding feral cats in a public or private location.

(B) In order to encourage spay/neuter of feral cats and to protect cats, public or private sheltering agencies or rescue groups shall not lend, rent, or otherwise provide traps to the public to capture cats, except to a person for the purpose of catching and reclaiming that person's wayward

cat(s), to capture injured or sick cats or cats otherwise in danger, to capture feral kittens for purposes of taming and adoption, or, in the case of
feral cats, for purposes of spay/neuter and subsequent re-release;
(1) For purposes of this subsection, the location of the cats, without more,
does not constitute "otherwise in danger";
(2) A person is subject to civil penalties of not less than two hundred dollars ($200) or more than five hundred dollars ($500) if that person uses
a trap from a public or private sheltering agency or rescue group for purposes other than those enumerated above.

(c) An action for a penalty proposed under this section may be commenced in a court of competent jurisdiction by the administrator of the
public or private animal sheltering agency or rescue group from which
the recipient obtained the trap that is the subject of the violation.

(d) All penalties collected under this section shall be retained by the
agency bringing the action under subsection (c) to be used solely for programs to spay or neuter animals.

Part V. Holding Periods.

SEC. 6(A) The required holding period for a stray animal impounded by
any public or private sheltering agency shall be five business days, not including the day of impoundment, unless otherwise provided in this section:
(1) Stray animals without any form of identification and without a known
owner shall be held for owner redemption during the first two days of the
holding period, not including the day of impoundment, and shall be
available for owner redemption, transfer, and adoption for the remainder of the holding period; (2) Stray animals may be adopted into new
homes or transferred to a rescue group or private sheltering agency for
the purpose of adoption after the first two days of the holding period, not
including the day of impoundment, except as provided in subsections (A)
(3) to (9);(3) If a stray animal is impounded with a license tag, microchip,
or other form of identification, or belongs to a known owner, the animal shall
be held for owner redemption during the first three days of the holding

period, not including the day of impoundment, and shall be available for owner redemption, transfer, and adoption for the remainder of the holding period; (4) Litters of animals or individual members of a litter of animals, including the nursing mother, and unweaned animals may be transferred to a private sheltering agency or rescue group for the purpose of adoption immediately after impound; (5) Individual members of litters of animals who are at least six weeks of age, including the mother, may be adopted immediately upon impound; (6) A feral cat caregiver has the same right of redemption for feral cats as an owner of a pet cat, without conferring ownership of the cat(s) on the caregiver; (7) Irremediably suffering animals shall be euthanized without delay, upon a determination made in writing and signed by a veterinarian licensed to practice medicine in this state. That certification shall be made available for free public inspection for no less than three years; (8) Symptomatic dogs with confirmed cases of parvovirus or cats with confirmed cases of panleukopenia may be euthanized without delay, upon a certification made in writing and signed by a veterinarian licensed to practice medicine in this state that the prognosis is poor even with supportive care. That certification shall be made available for free public inspection for no less than three years; (9) Unweaned animals impounded without their mother may be killed so long as the shelter has exhausted all efforts to place the animals in foster care, made an emergency appeal under the requirements of Section 9, and certified that it is unable to provide the needed care and feeding in its facility. That certification shall also state in clear and definitive terms why the agency is unable to place the animals in foster care, which private sheltering agencies and rescue groups it made an appeal to, and what would be required in the future in order to provide the needed care and feeding in foster care or its facility, and what steps are being taken to do so. This certification shall be made in writing, signed by the director of the agency or by a veterinarian, and be made available for free public inspection for no less than three years.

SEC. 7(A) The required holding period for an owner relinquished animal impounded by public or private sheltering agencies shall be the same as that for stray animals and applies to all owner relinquished animals, except as follows:(1) Any owner-relinquished animal that is impounded shall be held for adoption or for transfer to a private sheltering agency or rescue group for the purpose of adoption for the entirety of the holding period;(2) Owner-relinquished animals may be adopted into new homes or transferred to a private sheltering agency or rescue group for the purpose of adoption at any time after impoundment.

(B) When an animal is surrendered or brought to a shelter to be killed at the owner's request, the animal shall be subject to the same holding periods and the same requirements of all owner relinquished animals notwithstanding the request.

(c) An animal seized by an officer of a public or private sheltering agency under the provisions of a state statute having as its effect the prevention or punishment of animal neglect or cruelty, or seized under the provision of state dangerous dog laws or under state quarantine or disease control regulations, shall be impounded and held as consistent with the requirements of those laws, except as follows:

(1) Where any statute under the provisions of those laws permits a holding period, care, or disposition which affords an animal less protection than the mandates of this Act, this Act shall supersede those specific provisions regarding holding, care, and disposition.

Part VI. Animal Care Standards.

SEC. 8(A) Except as otherwise provided in this section, public and private sheltering agencies shall provide all animals during the entirety of their shelter stay with fresh food; fresh water; environmental enrichment to promote their psychological well-being such as socialization, toys and treats; and exercise as needed; however, never less than once daily, except as follows:

(1) dogs who are vicious to people or dangerous dogs may but are not required to be exercised during the holding period.

(B) Notwithstanding subsection (A), public and private sheltering agencies shall work with a veterinarian licensed to practice medicine in this state to develop and follow a care protocol, which is consistent with the goals of this Act as defined in Part I, for animals with special needs such as, but not limited to, nursing mothers, unweaned animals, sick or injured animals, geriatric animals, or animals needing therapeutic exercise. This care protocol shall specify any deviation from the standard requirements of subsection (A) and the reasons for the deviation(s).

(c) During the entirety of their shelter stay, animals shall be provided prompt and necessary cleaning of their cages, kennels, or other living environments no less than two times per day, to ensure environments that are welcoming to the public, hygienic for both the public and animals, and to prevent disease. This cleaning shall be conducted in accordance with a protocol developed in coordination with a veterinarian licensed to practice medicine in this state, provided as follows:

(1) animals shall be temporarily removed from their cages, kennels, or other living environments during the process of cleaning, to prevent them from being exposed to water from hoses or sprays, cleaning solutions, detergents, solvents, and/or chemicals.

(D) During the entirety of their shelter stay, all animals shall be provided with prompt and necessary veterinary care, including but not limited to preventative vaccinations, cage rest, fluid therapy, pain management, and/or antibiotics, sufficient to alleviate any pain caused by disease or injury, to prevent a condition from worsening, and to allow them to leave the shelter in reasonable condition, even if the animals are not candidates for redemption, transfer, or adoption.

(E) Public and private sheltering agencies shall work with a veterinarian licensed to practice medicine in this state to develop and follow a protocol to prevent the spread of disease, including, but not limited to, appropriate evaluation and testing of newly impounded animals, administration of vaccines, proper isolation and handling of sick animals, and measures to protect those animals most vulnerable to infection.

Part VII. Additional Programs and Duties.

SEC. 9(A) All public and private sheltering agencies that kill animals shall maintain a registry of organizations willing to accept animals for the purposes of adoption, as follows: (1) All public or private sheltering agencies, and rescue groups designated as non-profits by Section 501(c)(3) of the Internal Revenue Code, shall be immediately placed on this registry upon their request, regardless of the organizations' geographical location or any other factor except as described under subsection (A)(5); (2) The public or private sheltering agency may, but is not required to, include on the registry any rescue groups that are not designated as non-profits under Section 501(c)(3) of the Internal Revenue Code; (3) The registry shall include the following information as provided by the registered organization: organization name, mailing address, and telephone number; website and e-mail address, if any; emergency contact information for the organization; the types of animals about whom the organization wishes to be contacted, including species-type and breed; and whether or not the organization is willing and able to care for unweaned animals, sick or injured animals, and/or feral or aggressive animals; (4) All public and private sheltering agencies shall seek organizations to include on the registry; (5) A public or private sheltering agency may refuse to include an organization on the registry, or delete it from the registry, until such time as this is no longer the case, if any of the organization's current directors and/or officers have been convicted in a court of competent jurisdiction of a crime consisting of cruelty to animals or neglect of animals; or if such charges are pending against any of the organization's current directors or officers; or if that organization or its current directors or officers are constrained by a court order or legally binding agreement that prevents the organization from taking in or keeping animals. An agency may require an organization to disclose any or all convictions, charges, and legal impediments described in this subsection; (6) A public or private sheltering agency may require that registered organizations provide the following summary information on no more than a monthly basis: the total number of animals the organization has taken from the agency who have been adopted, died, were transferred, were killed, and are still under the organization's care. This information may be provided in an informal format, such as via electronic mail; (7) A public or private sheltering agency shall not demand additional information, other than that described in this section, as a prerequisite for including an organization on the registry or for continuing to maintain that organization on the registry.

(B) No public or private sheltering agency may kill an animal unless and until the agency has notified, or made a reasonable attempt to notify, all organizations on the registry described in subsection (A) that have indicated a willingness to take an animal of that type.

(1) Such notification must take place at least two business days prior to the killing of the animal; (2) At a minimum, such notification shall include calling the organization's regular and emergency contact numbers, and sending an email to its email address, if any. Notification is considered complete as to each individual group when this has been accomplished; (3) No animal may be killed if an organization on the registry is willing and able to take the animal within two business days after being notified; (4) No fee may be assessed for animals released to organizations listed on the registry.

(c) No public or private sheltering agency may kill an animal unless and until the agency has notified, or made a reasonable attempt to notify, individual rescuers, rescue groups who are not designated as a non-profit under Section 501(c)(3) of the Internal Revenue Service, and the public at large so that they may consider adopting or rescuing the animal consistent with the agency's normal adoption or transfer protocols.

(1) Such notification must take place at least two business days prior to the killing of the animal; (2) Such notification can be accomplished in any manner reasonably likely to lead to lifesaving, but must, at a minimum, include posting a notice in the shelter on the particular animal's cage or kennel, and on the agency's website that states: "This animal is to be killed on [date] and [time]."

(D) The following exceptions shall apply to the requirements of subsections (B) and (c):

(1) All irremediably suffering animals shall be euthanized without delay. The determination that an animal is irremediably suffering shall be made in writing, signed by a veterinarian licensed to practice medicine in this state, and made available for free public inspection for no less than three years; (2) Symptomatic dogs with confirmed cases of parvovirus or cats with confirmed cases of panleukopenia may be euthanized without delay, upon a certification made in writing and signed by a veterinarian licensed to practice medicine in this state that the prognosis is poor even with supportive care. Such certification shall be made available for free public inspection for no less than three years; (3) Dangerous dogs may, but are not required to be, released to organizations listed on the registry; (4) Upon the impoundment of unweaned animals without their mother, all public and private sheltering agencies which have not placed the animals into foster care or are not able to provide supplemental feeding shall immediately make an emergency appeal to organizations on the registry that have indicated that they are willing and able to care for unweaned animals, and give such organizations a reasonable amount of time to respond to the appeal. Unweaned animals impounded without their mother may then be killed before the expiration of the two business days notification period if the requirements of Section 6(A)(9) are met.

(E) All public and private sheltering agencies shall require organizations taking animals under this section to sign a contract providing:

(1) That the animals are being taken for the purposes of adoption;(2) That all animals taken from the agency will be spayed or neutered before adoption, unless a licensed veterinarian certifies that an animal is too sick to be spayed or neutered or that it would otherwise be detrimental to the health of the animal to be spayed or neutered as required under Section 3 of this Act.

SEC. 10(A) All public and private sheltering agencies shall take appropriate action to ensure that all animals are checked for all currently acceptable methods of identification, including microchips, identification tags, and licenses. All public and private sheltering agencies shall maintain continuously updated lists of animals reported lost, and match these lost reports with animals reported found and animals in the shelter, and shall also post all stray animals on the Internet with sufficient detail to allow them to be recognized and claimed by their owners. If a possible owner is identified, the agencies shall undertake reasonable efforts to notify the owner or caretaker of the whereabouts of the animal and any procedures available for the lawful recovery of the animal. These efforts shall include, but are not limited to, notifying the possible owner by telephone, mail, and personal service to the last known address. Upon the owner's or caretaker's initiation of recovery procedures, the agencies shall retain custody of the animal for a reasonable period of time to allow for completion of the recovery process. Efforts to locate or contact an owner or caretaker, and communications with persons claiming to be owners or caretakers, shall be recorded and be made available for free public inspection for no less than three years.

SEC. 11(A) Every public or private sheltering agency shall have adoption programs which include adoption programs to place animals into homes and to transfer animals to other private sheltering agencies or rescue groups for adoption; promotion of animals to the community through means such as the local media and the Internet; evening and weekend adoption hours; and, community-based adoption events or venues at locations other than the shelter.

(1) In addition to the requirements of subsection (A), all public sheltering agencies shall be open for public adoption seven days per week for a minimum of six hours per day, except on the following federally recognized holidays, when the shelter may, but is not required to, be open for adoptions: Thanksgiving Day and Christmas Day.

SEC. 12(A) No public or private sheltering agency shall ban, bar, limit or otherwise obstruct the adoption of any animal based on arbitrary criteria, such as breed, age, color, or any other criteria except as to the individual animal's medical condition and aggression, or the adopter's fitness to adopt.

SEC. 13(A) Every public sheltering agency shall provide the following public services:(1) low-cost spay/neuter services for animals;(2) volunteer opportunities for people to assist the shelter, including fostering animals, socializing animals, assisting with adoptions, and otherwise helping in the operations of the shelter;(3) programs to assist people in overcoming situations that may cause them to relinquish or abandon their animals, including, but not limited to, programs that address animal behavior problems, medical conditions, and environmental conditions.

(B) Nothing in this section shall prohibit an agency from enacting reasonable rules to facilitate the orderly operation of these programs, so long as the rules are designed to meet the goals of this Act, as defined in Part I.

SEC. 14(A) No person shall procure or use any living animal from a public or private sheltering agency or rescue group for medical or biological teaching, research or study. No hospital, educational or commercial institution, laboratory, or animal dealer, whether or not such dealer is licensed by the United States Department of Agriculture, shall purchase or accept any living animal from a public or private sheltering agency, rescue group, commercial kennel, kennel, peace officer, or animal control officer.

(B) No public or private sheltering agency, rescue group, commercial kennel, kennel, peace officer, or animal control officer shall sell, adopt, transfer, or give away any living animal to a person, hospital, educational or commercial institution, laboratory, or dealer in animals, whether or not such dealer is licensed by the United States Department of Agriculture, for purposes of medical or biological teaching, research or study.

SEC. 15(A) No savable animal in a public or private sheltering agency shall be killed simply because the holding period has expired. Before an animal is killed, all of the following conditions must be met:
(1) there are no empty cages, kennels, or other living environments in the shelter; (2) the animal cannot share a cage or kennel with another animal; (3) a foster home is not available; (4) organizations listed on the registry described in Section 9 are not willing to accept the animal; (5) the animal is not a feral cat subject to sterilization and release; (6) all

mandates, programs and services of the Act have been met; and (7) the director of the agency certifies he or she has no other alternative.

(B) The determination that all conditions of subsection (a) have been met shall be made in writing, signed by the director of the agency, and be made available for free public inspection for no less than three years.

SEC. 16(A) All animals impounded by a public or private sheltering agency or rescue group shall be killed, only when necessary and consistent with the requirements of this Act, by lethal intravenous injection of sodium pentobarbital, except as follows:

(1) intraperitoneal injections may be used only under the direction of a licensed veterinarian, and only when intravenous injection is not possible for infant animals, companion animals other than cats and dogs, feral cats, or in comatose animals with depressed vascular function. (2) intracardiac injections may be used only when intravenous injection is not possible for animals who are completely unconscious or comatose, and then only under the direction of a veterinarian.

(B) No animal shall be allowed to witness any other animal being killed or being tranquilized/sedated for the purpose of being killed or see the bodies of animals which have already been killed.

(C) Animals shall be sedated/tranquilized as necessary to minimize their stress or discomfort, or in the case of vicious animals, to ensure staff safety, except as follows:

(1) neuromuscular blocking agents shall not be used.

(D) Following their injection, animals shall be lowered to the surface on which they are being held and shall not be permitted to drop or otherwise collapse without support.

(E) An animal may not be left unattended between the time procedures to kill the animal are commenced and the time death occurs, nor may the body be disposed of until death is verified.

(F) Verification of death shall be confirmed for each animal in all of the following ways:
(1) by lack of heartbeat, verified by a stethoscope; (2) by lack of respiration, verified by observation; (3) by pale, bluish gums and tongue, verified by observation; and (4) by lack of eye response, verified if lid does not blink when eye is touched and pupil remains dilated when a light is shined on it.

(G) The room in which animals are killed shall be cleaned and regularly disinfected as necessary, but no less than once per day on days the room is used, except as follows:
(1) The area where the procedure is performed shall be cleaned and disinfected between each procedure.

(H) The room in which animals are killed shall have adequate ventilation that prevents the accumulation of odors.

(I) A veterinarian licensed to practice medicine in this state or a euthanasia technician certified by the state euthanasia certification program shall perform these procedures, except as follows:
(1) If a state certification program does not exist, the procedure may be performed by a trained euthanasia technician working under the direction of a veterinarian.

Part VIII. Public Accountability.

SEC. 17(A) All public and private sheltering agencies must post, in a conspicuous place where animals are being relinquished by owners, a sign which is clearly visible and readable from any vantage point in the area, and at least 17 inches by 22 inches, which has all of the following information identified by species-type:
(1) the number of animals impounded for the prior calendar year; (2) the number of animals impounded for the prior calendar year who were adopted; (3) the number of animals impounded for the prior calendar year

who were transferred to other agencies for adoption;(4) the number of animals impounded for the prior calendar year who were reclaimed by their owners; (5) the number of animals impounded for the prior calendar year who died, were lost, and/or were stolen while under the direct or constructive care of the agency; and (6) the number of animals impounded for the prior calendar year who were killed by the agency, at the agency's direction, with the agency's permission, and/or by a representative of the agency.

(B) All public or private sheltering agencies must provide all owners who are relinquishing an animal with accurate information, in writing, about the likely disposition of their animal which includes, but is not limited to: (1) if the animal is the breed or type who is normally killed, (2) if the animal is likely to be killed because of some current, usual, or unusual circumstances, and (3) the information provided in Section 17(A)(1)-(6).

(c) Any owner surrendering an animal to a public or private sheltering agency must sign a statement on a form provided by the agency which includes the specific language: "I understand that the shelter may kill my pet." If such statements are provided on a form which has additional information, the owner must initial the statement where these words appear. If the person refuses to sign such statement, the shelter, or its agents, must recite the statement aloud to the owner and then write: "Refused to sign." Such statements must be kept on file for a period of no less than three years.

(D) All public and private sheltering agencies must make available for free public inspection the care protocol required under Section 8(B), the cleaning protocol required under Section 8(c), and the disease-prevention protocol required under Section 8 (E).

(E) All public and private sheltering agencies shall include on their websites and post, in a conspicuous place near the entrance of the shelter, a list of organizations included on the registry described in Section 9, as well as an invitation for all public or private sheltering agencies and rescue groups to inquire about being listed on the registry, so that they may be notified before any animal is killed. Such lists shall not include any contact information the registered organizations do not wish to make public.

SEC. 18(A) All public or private sheltering agencies shall provide to the City Council and, upon request, for free public inspection, a monthly summary by the tenth day of the month that includes the following information by species-type:

(1) the number of animals impounded during the previous month; (2) the number of impounded animals sterilized and/or sterilized by contract with participating outside private veterinarians during the previous month; (3) the number of animals who were killed by the agency, at the agency's direction, with the agency's permission, and/or by a representative of the agency during the previous month; (4) the number of animals who died, were lost, and/or were stolen while in the direct or constructive care of such agency during the previous month; (5) the number of animals who were returned to their owners during the previous month; (6) the number of animals who were adopted during the previous month; (7) the number of animals who were transferred to other organizations for adoption during the previous month; and (8) the number of animals impounded into the reporting agency from outside the city during the previous month.

(B) Every public or private sheltering agency shall provide an annual summary by January 31 to the City Council and, upon request, for free public inspection, which includes the following information by species-type:

(1) the number of animals impounded during the previous calendar year; (2) the number of impounded animals sterilized and/or sterilized by contract with participating outside private veterinarians during the previous calendar year; (3) the number of animals who were killed by the agency, at the agency's direction, with the agency's permission, and/or by a representative of the agency during the previous calendar year; (4) the number of animals who died, were lost, and/or were stolen while in the direct or constructive care of such agency during the previous

calendar year;(5) the number of animals who were returned to their owners during the previous calendar year;(6) the number of animals who
were adopted during the previous calendar year; (7) the number of animals
who were transferred to other organizations for adoption during the previous calendar year; and (8) the number of animals impounded into the
reporting agency from outside the city during the previous calendar
year.

SEC. 19(A) Revenues from dog licenses, as required under any existing
state or local laws, shall be deposited into an account for use by the public
animal control agency as follows: (1) 60 percent shall be used exclusively
for free and low-cost spay/neuter of feral cats and owned animals under
the provision of subsection (B);(2) 40 percent shall be used exclusively for
free and low-cost medical assistance, including vaccinations, of feral cats
and owned animals under the provision of subsection (B).

(B) These funds shall be used to provide low-cost spay/neuter and medical care for animals if the owner or feral cat caretaker meets income
guidelines set by the shelter or city except as follows:
(1) These funds shall be used to provide free spay/neuter for animals if
the owner is on public assistance or is eligible for any type of city, county,
state, or federal aid of the kind that is normally given to individuals based
on lack of sufficient income; (2) These funds shall be used to provide
low-cost medical care, including vaccinations, for animals if the owner is
on public assistance or is eligible for any type of city, county, state, or
federal aid of the kind that is normally given to individuals based on lack
of sufficient income; (3) These funds shall be used to provide free spay/
neuter and vaccinations against rabies for feral cats regardless of the feral cat caretaker's income.

(c) These services shall be performed under the direction of a licensed
veterinarian.

(D) These funds shall not be deducted from the public animal control
agency's overall city budget.

SEC. 20(A) Any resident of the city may compel a public or private sheltering agency or rescue group to follow the mandates of this Act through a lawsuit asking a court of competent jurisdiction to grant declaratory and injunctive relief including, but not limited to: restraining orders, preliminary injunctions, injunctions, writs of mandamus and prohibition, and other appropriate remedies at law which will compel compliance with this Act.

(B) Any public or private sheltering agency or rescue group may compel a public or private sheltering agency to follow the mandates of this Act through a lawsuit asking a court of competent jurisdiction to grant declaratory and injunctive relief including, but not limited to: restraining orders, preliminary injunctions, injunctions, writs of mandamus and prohibition, and other appropriate remedies at law which will compel compliance with this Act.

SEC. 21(A) Any law, ordinance, or policy which requires the licensing of cats, the confinement of cats, limits the number of animals a household can own or care for, prohibits or requires permits for the feeding of stray domestic animals, or prohibits the adoption of specific breeds of dogs is hereby repealed as contrary to the public interest except as follows:

(1) Nothing in this section shall be construed to limit the enforcement of a statute having as its effect the prevention or punishment of animal neglect or cruelty, so long as such enforcement is based on the conditions of animals or the environment, and not based on the mere fact that a household has a certain number of animals, a person is feeding stray domestic animals, and/or a dog is of a particular breed.

SEC. 22(A) If the provisions of any article, section, subsection, paragraph, subdivision or clause of this Act shall be adjudged invalid by a court or other tribunal of competent jurisdiction, such determination, order, or judgment shall not affect or invalidate the remainder of any article, section, subsection, paragraph, subdivision or clause of this Act. Any such invalidity shall be confined in its operation to the clause, sentence, paragraph, section or article thereof directly involved in the controversy in which such determination, order, or judgment shall have been rendered.

Acknowledgments

I WANT TO THANK my wife, Jennifer, whose input, revisions, and exhortations that we can always do more as a society compel me to ask for more as a writer and as an advocate for animals. I also want to thank Mike Fry and Beth Nelson of Animal Wise Radio for giving me a forum to share my views with a national radio audience. Many of the essays in this book started as discussions with Mike and Beth in our weekly segment.

I must thank Susan Cosby for building a website for me, and pulling me kicking and screaming into 21st century media such as blogs and twitter, which has opened up new groups of people to convert to the No Kill cause. I am indebted to my editors: Barbara Saunders, Michael Baus, and Marc Baldwin and his team. But most of all, I want to thank the public—the dog and cat loving American public.

When I first began my work in the animal rights movement some 20 years ago, I was overwhelmed when I learned about the widespread killing and abuse of animals in various contexts. I was bitter and tended to believe that people were uncaring and cruel. My indignation was fueled by the daily dose of bad news I received through my work in animal protection. I lived in the trenches, and as can often happen when your vision is hindered in such a way, I became myopic. I focused primarily on the bad things people did to animals, and became blind to the good. As a result, I lost an accurate perspective. I lost the ability to perceive how most people really feel about animals, and with that, a sense of the animal protection movement's potential for success.

But then something happened that changed me. When I began to focus my efforts on ending shelter killing, I began to see a different side of the story—a more positive, hopeful, and I now believe, accurate measure of humanity. Through my work in the No Kill movement, I have encountered people from all walks of life—every demographic imaginable: every age, class, culture, and political leaning—united, in spite of their other differences, by their love and concern for animals. I have witnessed, time and time again, how the public rallies to the call for reform of their local shelter, and how, with their assistance, No Kill is now succeeding in various and diverse communities across this country.

I also came to see how this transcends companion animals as well: the passage of Proposition 2 in California to ban some of the cruelest conditions in factory farms, and the growth and mainstreaming of vegetarian restaurants, vegetarian foods, and cruelty-free and environmentally-friendly products.

These experiences have combined to erode my despair and replace it with great optimism. They have helped me understand that when it comes to protecting animals, the battle is against the few who have a vested interest in the status quo; rather than the many, who will reject cruelty and killing and embrace compassion when they are given the information which allows them to see it clearly for what it is, and when a path to a more humane future is cleared before them. Sadly, the leadership of today's animal protection movement refuses to recognize this potential and therefore, refuses to act upon it. But, more tragically, they are threatened when others do.

Quoting historian John Barry, I wrote in *Redemption* that "institutions reflect the cumulative personalities of those within them, especially their leadership. They tend, unfortunately, to mirror less admirable human traits, developing and protecting self-interest and even ambition." They try to create order, not by learning from others or the past, but "by closing off and isolating themselves from that which does not fit. They become bureaucratic." One of the fundamental downsides of bureaucracies is their focus on self-preservation at the expense of their mission. And in the case of animal shelters and the national allies who support them, this bureaucracy kills animals. But the leaders of HSUS, PETA, and others are fighting a losing battle to stop the No Kill revolution from destroying every last vestige of the "catch and kill" paradigm they protect, because we have the hearts and minds of the public on our side.

And I am constantly reminded of how much people truly love animals: From donating tens of millions of dollars when animals are impacted by a disaster to the great lengths taken to care for their own pets; from rising to the challenge when their local shelter commits itself to a No Kill goal, to voting for animal protection legislation even when all the powers-that-be tell them doing so will hurt their own economic interests; and, in countless little ways. Recently, for example, I was standing next to an older gentleman at a pharmacy when I asked the clerk for lancets for my diabetic cat. Lancets are used for diabetic testing. It's the device that punctures the skin to extract blood for monitoring. When the pharmacist asked me what kind I wanted, I said to "give me the *finest* you have because it is for my cat." The gentleman turned to me, pumped his fist in the air, and said to the pharmacist: "Yes, give him the finest, because nothing is too good for our pets!" I smiled at him and said, "That is true. Nothing is too good for our pets." But when I said "finest," I actually meant "fine" as in the smallest needle point or highest gauge because the blood was drawn from the cat's ear and I did not want it to be painful. Nonetheless, experiences like that, which I encounter frequently, remind me just how widespread our love for companion animals is as a society.

And it is that love that gives me faith that we will fix our broken animal shelter system. Ultimately, not only will we save lives; but we will also create a future where every animal will be respected and cherished, and where every individual life will be protected and revered.

About the Author

Nathan J. Winograd is a graduate of Stanford Law School, and is both a former criminal prosecutor and corporate attorney. An ethical vegan and lifelong animal rescuer, his passion has always been helping animals, and he left the law to dedicate himself to that task. He has helped write animal protection legislation at the state and national level, has spoken nationally and internationally on animal sheltering issues, has created successful No Kill programs in both urban and rural communities, and has consulted with a wide range of animal protection groups, including some of the largest and best known in the nation. Under his leadership, Tompkins County, New York became the first No Kill community in the United States. He has since helped many others achieve the same success. His first book, *Redemption: The Myth of Pet Overpopulation & The No Kill Revolution in America*, won five national book awards and redefined the animal protection movement nationwide. He lives in the San Francisco Bay Area with his wife, two children, and a menagerie of animal companions. For more information, visit www.nathanwinograd.com.